# ANCHOR BOOKS

# THE MAGIC OF LOVE

First published in Great Britain in 1995 by
ANCHOR BOOKS
1-2 Wainman Road, Woodston,
Peterborough, PE2 7BU

SB ISBN 1 85930 062 6

# *Foreword*

Anchor Books is a small press, established in 1992, with the aim of promoting readable poetry to as wide an audience as possible.

We hope to establish an outlet for writers of poetry who may have struggled to see their work in print.

The poems presented here have been selected from many entries. Editing proved to be a difficult and daunting task and as the Editor, the final selection was mine.

The poems chosen represent a cross-section of styles and content. They have been sent from all over the world, written by young and old alike, united in the passion for writing poetry.

I trust this selection will delight and please the authors and all those who enjoy reading poetry.

Andrew Head
Editor

# CONTENTS

## COURIER

Partners whose prowess ascends to an art
are skilled in the pleasures of love.
Awakening the innocent -
- body and mind -
with a sweetness of touch,
feather gentle and kind.
Sharing a gift in the warmth of a gaze.
Knowing the value of simple embrace.

*Mandy Rossiter*


## LOVE HURTS!

Are you really worth
the pain that I go through?
Because every single day
I hurt more and more for you.
I think you're very special
but you don't know I care
And every time I'm with you
these feelings are always there.
I see you every day
with a smile upon your face
And every time I leave you
from my mind I can't erase.
You are always in my thoughts
you never go away
Every time I try to tell you
I don't know what to say.
I know we'll never be together
you're far too good for me
Four words I know I'll never say
are 'You belong to me!'

*Diana Mitchell*

## ALEXANDER MY GREAT

I love the way the rain comes sweeping down across the moor.
I love the way the waves come pounding on the shore.
I love the colours of the rainbow, when it glows twixt sun and rain
I love the power of your smile, which helps drive away my pain.
I still love the sight and sound of you, just as on the day we met,
I'll love you Alex to eternity, when our last sun has set.

*Freda Barnett Harman*


## REFLECTIVE - CONTEMPLATION

When pausing to relax, at some point of the day,
*quietly hushed* in privacy of our own,
I use this precious time to communicate and say:-

'How nice it is together - alone!' -

To be able to contemplate on memories past
whilst talking and enjoying a drink;
a chance *to-work-things-out* and think . . .

Love is so nice at times like these,
particularly *when caught in a passionate squeeze;*
kisses so warm and tender are good

(wondering now, if one shouldn't or should!)

But the *crescendo* will come eventually
and it could be fantastic, if you want it to be . . .!
Please, go on loving me - eternally -

*D A Spence-Crawford*

## DO YOU REMEMBER?

Do you remember the times long ago?
Driving through snowy winter lanes, through tunnels of white hedges,
You smiling fondly, hand up my skirt,
I smiling back, happy to be driven,
Safe and cosseted - like a child, loved unconditionally.

Later, Norfolk log fires,
Toasting toast, and getting burnt,
Starship's 'Nothing's going to stop us now',
Dancing together in the dark.

Later still - moving in,
Stripping doors, and door frames whilst you were away,
Airport leavings, and meetings,
Travelling down in the fog.

Do I remember the sick excitement? - trying to fix my hair,
Sexy suspenders, and the latest perfume - seems so long ago,
I never recognised you at the airport,
My mind's eye never matched the reality - until you spoke.

Then the embarrassed journey home,
Making polite conversation, until we were able to couple together,
To destroy the barriers,
Able to be as one again.

Seems so long ago, we gave into our emotions,
Instead of fighting them off,
Relaxed into the acceptance of our needs,
Instead of denying them, in favour of practical things.

Can we go back, do you think?
Forget the ironing, and remember the kissing,
Show our children that we are lovers - not care assistants?
Indulge, and nurture our feelings, and grow,
Relax and love? Relax and love!

*Susan Thompson*

## LAY DOWN

Lay your soul down on me

Let me hold it safe in my arms
while you return to it
after a little
from where your mind has wandered far
and roamed through time, space, place
and touch.

And lay your strong shoulders and your soft head
down on me
Here I'll hold you safe forever
within this circle of frail arms,
mother you as mother our children.

Broad man, I love you,
lay your soul down.

*Eileen S Cowey*


## IF

If the stars were all to fall down from the sky,
If the birds all ceased to sing way up on high,
If the rivers all ran dry,
If the extrovert turned shy,
If the sun no longer shone,
If they dropped the atomic bomb,
If the truthful were untrue,
If no flowers ever grew,
As long as there's we two,
I'll still be loving you.

*Allison Magee*

## LOVERS

Such is the depth you seek in me
My very soul melts to meet you.
The hard core of every day between us
Fuses and turns to liquid gold.
The salty tears of our flesh mingle
And blend into the musky scents of lust.
Even the leaves dapple your skin
With their kindness to shield you
From the burning heat of noon.

If we were young, this would be love!
We would sigh and mourn for
Wasted hours and lost chances.
But we are in high summer,
Have seen the wilted flowers of spring
Drooping in the high grasses.
When the season of heat is so short
And autumn but the road to grey winter,
We grieve only the passing months
And count each panting breath a bonus.

When frost comes
And snow flurries on the hills
When cows low for the byre
And birds have long gone south,
Our hands will drift apart,
Eyes peer into the distance
For all that is familiar
Comforting and warm
And we will go home.

*Mollie Wade*

## STICK TO THE FIGHT

Life deals everyone a tough card
And now and again life seems hard
You'll get through it
Bit by bit
Don't you worry
Don't you quit

When you're having a hard time
And the sun just doesn't seem to shine
Buck up
Look up
See the sun
Don't give in
One day you'll win.

*Caroline Calvert*

## I LOVE YOU

It's as though my heart has been refreshed,
Filled with a beauty of new,
My whole body shakes at the thought of your name,
And the picture I've created of you.

You're so alive and seem so free,
Your kiss goodnight, encapsulates me,
And when I whisper in your ear,
The three main words aren't spoke with fear,

I love you more than the day we met,
Without a lie, without regret,
Before I kiss you, if I were to forget,
You are my life, my eternal breath.

*Philip May*

## MY WORLD

My world is you,
Each moment together
Is as special and fresh
As the morning dew.
Each touch - like a silken thread
Leaving behind a bond
Never to be broken.
Each tender look - a caress
And locked within my heart
Forever blest.
The years have flown
And we have grown together
Ever closer.
Our love has deepened
And will last forever.
Our vows - solemn and sincere
Have strengthened
And personified each year.
And so my love
As we tread life's way,
May each succeeding year
Be as wonderful
As you are to me today.

*Anne Baker*

## SO SWEET

The only person I've ever loved is you,
I'm telling you this, because it's true,
Don't think me all soppy simple and wet,
Or like something disgusting, like a cigarette.

At times you are so remote,
And I long to race to your heart like a speedboat,
Being without you, is so much pain,
I wish we could be together again.

A love like ours should be united,
Where all the wrongs in our love would be righted,
We could go to Jamaica, and lay on the beach,
And play with the children with whom we could teach.

We'd walk and talk on the beach you and I,
Then swim in the sea and towel ourselves dry,
But if anything happened to you and you die,
Well I would join you instantly in the sky.

*Ian Christopher*

## JUST A WORD

Whisper sweet nothings
To me in my ear,
Make me feel good
That it's worth being here,
Praise me a little, as
It pleases my mind,
Then happiness will last
Leaving troubles behind.

*Phyllis Wright*

# I LOVE THE WAY . . .

I think, perhaps, even though I don't say it you know I love you
But just how much you don't seem to realise,
How much it means to hear you say 'I've missed you' or 'I love you,'
To know you love me the way I am, no false pretences, no disguise.
I love the way you whisper your tender thoughts to me when we're alone
And the way you let me know you're still there by gently squeezing my hand.
I love the way your eyes speak to me and tell me secrets
So no one else knows or understands.
I love the way you kiss away my tears when I am hurting
And the way you too feel sad when I am down.
I love knowing that my happiness is your happiness
And that you miss me when I'm not around.
You mean more than the world to me
You're my very dream come true
And it wouldn't matter how strong I was
I know I could never live without you.
Your laughter is my laughter
Your grief and adversity is all mine too
For I can't help but feel what you're feeling
You intrigue me and I love you.
I love you so much I'd hold this world up if it was falling down on you.
I could never leave you feeling alone or in despair
And in your darkest hour I'd bring the sun to sit beside you
But if it couldn't, I would be there.
I love you more than I  ever thought possible
For you are the very seams which hold my soul together
You are my all, my everything
So here, take my heart, please keep it safe, for now, forever.

*Victoria Blake*

## LOVE IS ALL

When love is all
Caught in your throat
Like a lump
Or a perfect note

It makes you think
As you question why
Reality is always
A big white lie

Turning you daily
Inside out
With love and affection
And lots of doubt

Making you scream
All the more
As love wakes up
And you aren't quite sure

So lay down your dreams
And rest a while
Let some love
Try to bring a smile

As make believe
Takes on a glow
And you wrestle
With what you know

Before it turns
And kicks you again
Yes love is all
And this includes the pain

*Martin Booth*

10

## THE FEELING OF LOVE

A tingling feeling, deep down from within
is taunting and making my heart want to sing.
Melodies are rife, living inside my head,
it is difficult to sleep at night in my bed.

Life seems so magical, it is hard to explain,
the power and strength pumping around in my veins.
My heart is so happy, I feel I'm bursting with pride,
because I know that I am your guaranteed bride.

*Carol Ross*


## LILAC TREES

Do you ever think of me
When springtime sees the lilac tree,
And scented blossoms fill the air
When you and I were young and fair,
I see you now so tall and strong
Why did it have to go so wrong,
I loved you then as I do now
But time has passed since that last row.
You're married with a family
I wonder if you think of me,
It's twenty years since on that day
Our hopes and dreams were swept away.
But I still have sweet memories
Of youthful love and lilac trees.

*Margaret Malenoir*

## OUR SPECIAL LOVE

Over the years our love has grown,
It's like no other I've ever known.
We've both shared the good times and the bad,
We've both been happy and so sad.

I've trusted you throughout the years,
You've held me close and dried my tears.
You've taught me what I wanted to know,
You've helped our love to grow and grow.

The years have passed and here we stand,
Living a life that's really quite grand.
We'll stand by each other, we'll never part,
You hold that special place in my heart.

I love you more than words can say,
You are the one who shared each day.
When troubles arose, you stood close by,
I never heard one single sigh.

You've held me close every single night,
I've snuggled closer, when I've had a fright.
Your loving arms always encircled me,
I'm sure you'd never once disagree.

For you I'll do whatever I can,
You will always be my special man.
I'll stay by your side, right to the end.
You'll always be my special friend.

*Anne Cobb*

## SILK HANDCUFFS

I am the threshold of the unreal room
into which you quietly enter,
the centre of the murmuring undercurrent -
the suspect and the lure.

I am the foreplay, the traitor, the noose
the loose gangster's moll,
the cauldron of bubbling poetry
that overflows into your deepness.

I am the hush moving in your heat
the sweat beading your brow -
the reflections upon which you tread
as you try to regain your pace.

I am the silver space of drizzling stars
behind the questioning doorways of your eyes -
the precarious ledge where you
step out to seek your grip.

I am the perfume that awakens the senses,
the reeling memory of a past love -
the briar over the walled garden of
cherry blossom in which you hide.

I am the soft imprint on your skin
the thin whisper of handcuffs on silk -
I am the gamble in your stare
daring you to a new rendezvous

I am the quartz pathway climbing skyward
a heartbeat to snag your professional perfection -
I am the silent knock on illusion's door
bidding you play the music of dreams.

*Misty*

## LOVE'S SEASONS

The land is vernal green, and the country leaps to life;
The blackbird sings his poignant serenade;
On the bank, across the bridge, primroses run rife;
The chattering brook rills merrily through the glade.
Spring love has bewitching power, it wrapped us in its net,
Do you recall those days, my dear, when you and I first met?

Drowsy, droning honey bees around the hawthorn hedge,
A lark soars trilling to the cloudless sky,
A fallow deer trips warily down to the water's edge,
Out of the stillness a cuckoo's mournful cry.
Love alone can prosper through the simmering summer heat;
Do you recall our wedding when that love became complete?

The woods stretch out before us in their red and golden cloak;
The scent of burning stubble fills the air;
The busy squirrel seeks acorns from the gnarled roots of the oak,
And harvest mice are scampering everywhere.
Mellow wine is warm and rich, a taste to satisfy,
So our love grows sweeter as the autumn years roll by.

We've watched the seasons come and go, across the woodland stream;
Spring, Summer, Autumn - all have played their parts.
Although the northern winds are chill, our love will reign supreme,
And memories stay forever in our hearts.
We still dream together as the winter shadows fall,
For winter love's triumphant, the most beautiful of all.

*June Steele*

## A GIRL TO HER SOLDIER LOVER

David, do you remember as I do
   long nights of summer, when the soft, warm air
whispered among the birchwoods and we two
   wandered the lanes of Kent? A happy pair
we were, and saw the sickle moon
   fling silver magic from a dreaming sky
and never thought to lose it all so soon -
   the one to live alone, the one to die.

David, do you remember as you lie
   in that far grave which I shall never see
how once a single word, a single sigh
   could wake to golden flame your love for me?
How then it seemed a sudden, melting fire
   welded your lips to mine and breast to breast
joy in ecstatic striving of desire
   we found, and in love's consummation - rest.

Now all is ended and the empty years
   stretch on before me like an endless way
leading nowhere, and my bitter tears
   can find no comfort. Some have bid me pray
and talked to me of God and mocked my grief
   with tales of Providence and will not see
one thought alone can bring my heart relief -
   David, that you remember me.

*R P Fenwick*

15

## VALENTINE

Will you be mine? You wrote to me
many years ago
You didn't get down on one knee
didn't expect you to.

You were so many miles away
far across the sea
I didn't even hear you say
tender words to me.

It came by post, written in Greek
Translated it said
'I want to ask you something sweet
Will you marry me?'

I wrote straight back, of course I will
Hurry home to me
then we'll all our dreams fulfil
Together we will be.

Thirty six years together and
still your valentine
we are so happy and in love
I thank God, you're mine.

*Joan Berriman*

## ODE TO LOVE

You take your love away from me
But, my love for you can never be erased,
I see your face; within my head I hear your voice
It tumbles through my mind like musical bells tinkling in the breeze.

My heart is light, remembering shared laughter
But heavy with the suddenness of departing
And stark, like a tree bereft of golden leaves,
Words you spoke ring like echoes in my ear -
I see your fiery silken hair, your blue eyes ever crystal clear
And reminisce of every moment of fun
Sparkling hours of joy and sunshine gone for ever, except, within my heart
Where I hide the pain which pierces deep within, reaching every part.

O to hear the voice, as once I did
To see the smile lighting up grey days
To skip down country lanes without a care
To close my eyes, but know, that when I wake you will be there.

To love you, is to steal a fleeting moment out of time
But, as stars suspended from the heavens out of grasp and never mine,
Wherever at this moment you may be, peace fill your heart
Lightness keep your step, and, like a butterfly may you be flying free
And life unfold its wonders before you, precious, every one,
As you were, and are to me, until the days, the months and years,
The end of time, of every hour on earth shall come.

*Wendy A Cudd*

## SECRET LOVE

My love is locked within my heart.
a secret kept inside.
Although I dream of romance,
the feelings I have, I hide.

The one I love does not know
the way I feel about him,
because it's all a fantasy,
a true romantic dream.

In my mind I imagine
thoughts of love between us,
but in reality there is nothing
just emptiness, no us.

My heart it aches for love from you,
but that will never happen.
I wish that dreams could come true
and we could be an item.

But my heart it keeps the secret,
because you'll never be mine.
So my love remains inside, all locked,
and the feelings I just have to hide.

*Maggie Prickett*


## LIKEN MY LOVE

Liken my love to a rosebud ready to burst into bloom
The shine on her hair as the moonbeams cast adrift from the moon.
Liken her eyes of the deepest blue to a bluebell kissed by the dew
With a bouquet of English flowers my own true love I'll woo.

Liken her skin to a snowdrop as it bows its pure white head
While a tulip tints her gentle lips with barely a trace of red
Liken her cheeks to the sunset, a blush of the softest peach
With a bouquet of English flowers the heart of my love I'll reach.

Liken my love to the thistledown as it softly drifts on the breeze
Her scent to the orange blossom adorning summer's trees
Liken her heart to a lily, a pure and beautiful thing
With a bouquet of English flowers I'll offer her my ring.

*Sheila E Crathern*


## FOREVER

Entranced, I dreamily watched the warm elusive stream of honey
                                               dawn sunlight
Slowly slip her molten gold fingers through the open window of the
                                         peacefully still room,
And gingerly crawl her way to where you were sleeping - contented,
                                        innocent, beautiful.
Stroking the flawless perfection of your face,
I smiled as you softly sighed and gently rested against me
Like the wanton babe leans to the adoring mother -
So alluringly unaware of the overwhelming love I felt for you.
And, wholly enraptured in the light of this enviously fervent sun,
I recognised the true depth of immeasurable beauty,
The infinite strength of utmost devotion.
Silently watching you safely cradled in my arms,
On this wondrous new dawn,
I knew that you were deeply sealed within my heart;
Tenderly protected in the intensity of my very soul.
And there, you will always be,
Forever . . .

*Lynda Ann Green*

19

## YOUNG LOVE

Young love is so precious
It's like a breath of spring,
A touch of magic wonderment
Two hearts light, as bird on wing.

Tender sweet caresses,
Walking hand in hand,
Happy sharing thoughts and kisses
In this new found wonderland.

*Peggy Courteen*

## I O U

You said the first time
You looked into my eyes
You'd make me yours forever
You'd been taken by surprise
You'd never want another
You'd always be true
You swore to always love me.
You.

I seem to make you happy
I always try my best
I've always understood
I've not to be a pest
I've got to try and sparkle
I've not got to cry
I will always be here.
I.

*Emma Shaw*

## THE SPECIAL TREE

We wandered in the woods today listening.
To birds' choral sound,
leaves whispering,
murmuring from insects, bees humming
harmonies abound, all around.

We wandered in the woods today watching.
Branches rhythmic sway,
ancient canopy, timeless choreography.
It's said, counting trees inner rings gives
their age away.

We wandered in the woods today looking.
Found carved on mature bough,
words of love,
scratched in time.

We wandered in the woods today
remembering.
The special tree,
teenagers on a spree,
tentative smiles, that beguiled.

Ivy vine embraces now, names carved
destined to entwine.
finger tips retraced tenderly that pledge of
love,
Yours and mine.

*Joanne Manning*

## LIFE'S PEARL

Another year has passed, and still we are together
Through thick and thin, we have remained a couple
Our love has reached a higher plane
Now, we cannot be touched
Another year has, yet, to pass, and many more
We will persevere, to go on as one
With our minds and bodies combined
The world is our oyster
All we have to do, is find the pearl
That pearl, is the bond that holds hearts together

Perhaps, we have already found it . . .

*Graeme Lander*


## IF

If that we might be
One whole and perfect sky
I'd give to you
The golden sun
A pure eternal light

And if that we might be
One whole and perfect sky
Then let no cloud shed tears of rain
Yet let no rainbow die

And if the dawn should ever fail
Or the sunset cease to be
Then let the dark be lit with stars
And the love of you from me.

*John Forest Gaunt*

## MY OWN ONE

Take me across the sea ma laddie
Take me across the sea to Skye
Take me across the sea ma laddie
Where we will watch the Gaelic sun rise

I love thee how I love thee
With a love so rare and true
I love thee how I love thee
As the heather a-gleam with morning dew

Come with me to the glen and the loch
Walk with me in the faery mist
Come with me to the glen and the loch
Where all is tranquil and at rest

Take me across the sea ma laddie
Take me across the sea to Skye
In a wee boattie with Flora Macdonald
Ma bonnie laddie take me across to Skye

I long to tell thee how I love thee
I long to whisper words so sweetly
How I long to win you my own one
Midst the mountain ash in sight of the deer

I love thee how I love thee
With a love so rare and true
I love thee how I love thee
As the heather a-gleam with morning dew

*Margaret Bennett*

## HAPPY BIRTHDAY, DARLING

So age has caught up with you.
Why are you so sad? You should
Be counting all those blessings.
Darling, you have a job, a

Wife, a stepson, three dogs, a
Cat, three fish, a home, with the
Gardens almost as you'd like
Them. You are our TV kid.

Oh! I know, you are nearly
Bald, you'll never be a rich
Man, as one sees on TV
But my darling you are *loved.*

To be *loved*, to have a nice
And happy home, is what makes
This life so good. So darling
Just because, you are not so

Young any more, you like your
TV and have less hair, still
To grow old with you is what
I wish to do. So darling

*Happy Birthday, from the wife.*

**Norah Matter**

## PROGRAMMED

Even now I don't understand
How, when we met by merest chance,
The meeting seemed already planned.

Later that familiar touch
Of your hand in mine was something
Happening not for the first time but such

A very long time ago although
I didn't know when or where or why
And I didn't try to borrow

From the past when our tomorrow
Was written in light and sprinkled
With gold dust. When sorrow's shadow

Stared in our faces we shared
What no-one else dared comprehend:
Together in grief because we cared.

The shadow never went away
But it defined and underlined
The brightness of a gold-dust day.

Then the inexplicable touch
Of your familiar hand in mine
Had never before meant so much.

Where love is its powers prevail:
Like the configuration of stars
It is destined never to fail.

*Joan Board*

## NICKY

I never believed in love at first sight
Until you held me in your arms that night
Your touch, your smile, your kiss,
Are all the things that I now miss

The summer brought love and happiness
When it went it took you and left just emptiness
Now the winter's days are dark and long
I feel I'm on the edge just clinging on

Now I'm lying alone in my cold empty bed
With thoughts of you filling my head
Living without you is so hard to bear
My life means nothing without you there

I know you're not coming back and the hurt is hard to hide
I feel like I'm breaking up inside.
Everyone tells me that time will heal
But I know time could never change the way I feel

Memories don't fade away, they just grow deep
Reminding me of the love I couldn't keep
So this time Nicky I'll say goodbye for good
And hope to be with you again in heaven above.

*Amanda Johnson*


## MY WISH FOR YOU

At dawn the gentle dew descends
And earth at once is sweetly blessed;
So may our Lord's distilling grace
Lend to your suppliant spirit rest.

By noon the sun at zenith shines,
Source of all life each season through;
So may the light and love of God
Be shed abroad in your heart anew.

26

Each day the wind lifts cloud and bird
And breezes stir o'er land and sea;
So may you find yourself up-borne
With the wind of the Spirit blowing free.

Thus from the dew, the sun, the wind,
The soul can draw inspirational power;
So now I pray you may always know
That *still small voice* in the needful hour.

**Eileen King**


## TO RUBY

Though you are far away from me,
I see you in my dreams,
Your photograph stands by my bed
And you are here it seems.
Those days are gone when in my arms
We kissed and then caressed,
I held you tight, your hands in mine
Our hearts together pressed.
Those words you whispered tenderly
They were 'I love you dear'
They set my heart and soul alight
Those words I longed to hear.
That I loved you so very much
To you I tried to tell,
That without you life would be bleak
Consigned to live in Hell.
But you are far away my love,
I long so for your touch,
You are my love, you are my life,
I miss you Oh so much.

**William Francis**

## WITHIN MY HEART

When we first met
And fell in love,
I knew just what
You really meant to me;
For fate decreed
That you were mine,
And only mine,
Forever and a day.
Recalling now
Those bygone days
That seem so long ago,
And yet, they seem
To be like yesterday.
For I am sure
A cord of gold
Is still secure
Around the love
That holds us still,
And know that you
Will live always with me,
Within my heart,
Until Eternity;
My Joy,
My Life;
My Love,
My Wife;
My friend.

*H Val Horsfall*

## ACROSS THE SEA

On distant shores I stand and gaze,
out there to sea into the haze,
far o'er the ocean my homeland,
I dream, there standing on the sand,
the one I love, I hope and pray,
together soon, God speed the day,
blow wind across the sea,
whisper, my love please wait for me,
blow wind across the sea,
to where my heart so longs to be,
blow wind across the sea.

The twilight deepens, stars do shine,
please tell my love for her I pine,
then darkness falls, the moon appears,
she sees me standing mid my tears,
fly moon along the night,
please guide my love with love's own light,
fly moon across the sea,
to where my heart so longs to be,
fly moon along the night,
blow wind across the sea.

The silent clouds drift high in space,
I beg of them please haste their pace,
to tell you dear I miss you so,
how much I love you let you know,
roll clouds across the sky,
please say my love will never die,
roll clouds across the sea,
to where my heart so longs to be,
roll clouds across the sky
fly moon along the night
blow wind across the sea.

*J L Ord*

## HEAVEN SENT

The little thoughtful
       things you do
Make me fall in love
       with you.
When you smile
       and take my hand
It feels like Heaven
       it is so grand.
Your sense of humour
       you are so witty
You make me laugh
       till I am dizzy.
I thank the Lord up above
       for giving me you to love!

*Eda Singleton*


## LOVE SONG

I am the singer, you are my song;
the voice and the tune together belong.
You are the air I breathe and require;
yours is the heart and love I desire.

You are the singer, I am your song;
your voice and my theme together belong.
We breathe and sing our dual air
that celebrates the love we share.

The day that fate decreed, we met,
and sang the love song we never forget.

*Brian Chaplin*

## SWEET DREAMS

I hear your gentle
night time breathing
see the smile
that I put there
as one, we found
our Shangri La
I guess you know
you took me there
I watch you sleep
when passion's spent
and in your dreams
I hope I'm there
I feel the warmth
within your sleeping
reaching out
to still be there
and in the silence
of my thoughts
my quiet dreams
you're always there.

*Carole Jones*


## LOVELINESS

How can I give expression to
The thousand feelings I embrace?
So full am I that often I am dumb;
Your eyes defy the language of my art's device.

I dare no longer speak;
How cheap and crude do words at once appear,
When silence is a hymn more sweetly sung,
In praise of loveliness so pure.

*Phil Faulkner*

## A BRIGHTER FUTURE

Today the sun shines brighter
and the future seems so clear,
my heart feels so much lighter
and the unknown holds no fear.
The world in all its glory
seems perfect to me now,
it's just the age old story
of a true and loving vow.
The promise of a lover
to love forever more
and to cherish one another,
just makes my spirit soar.
To know we'll be together
with the love we have to share.
I hope it lasts forever
and that I'll always have you there.

*Lyn Ball*

## YOU HOLD THE KEY

You hold the key to all that I dream,
To take me away from all that has been.
The keeper of light to a passage that glows,
My exit my entrance to open new doors.
You are the one to unlock and release,
To awaken desires that's dormant in me.
A spark or a flicker, my custodian of light,
From a fire that's smouldering, only you could ignite,
You are my access, for you hold the key,
From a dark vacant space, to liberate me.

*Rita Improta*

## MYSTERIOUS STRANGER

The moon falls down beneath the sky.
Your feet gently grace the earth like a soft lullaby.
Your words tumble like soft ash onto the fire's hearth.
The flames breathe life to your lips.
One sensual kiss,
the moment drifts into a higher dimension.
Our love can never miss.

So take my hand, let yourself go,
There's no reason to be afraid.
You must know,
I'll protect you from danger.
My mysterious stranger.

There will never be a situation that you need to run from.
As solid as a rock.
I'll shield you from stronger rays beating down from the hottest sun.
Strength to strength,
I'll go to any length.
Like the wind that drives the waves,
we're on the crest of a natural reaction.
Heart to heart,
soul linked with soul.
We have the power of complete control.
You and me exist as not two but one,
as our thoughts become whole.

*Joanna Ashwell*

## TRUE LOVE

It does not seem so long ago
Though it's fifty years and more
Since you and I exchanged our vows
In nineteen forty four.

The first few years we spent apart
You were far away,
Serving in the Air Force
While I at home must stay.

Your duty done, you came back home
Life was like a song
We were content and happy
As our family came along

Sometimes things would go awry
Disappointments came our way
But we knew we'd conquer all
As long as we could say,

'I love you dear, with all my heart
You are the only one
Who can turn my darkness into light
And bring along the sun.'

Now we are in our autumn time
The children have flown the nest,
It's you and I together love
We've stood life's greatest tests

We've seen the wrinkles start to form
We've watched our hair turn grey
But our love has never faltered
As we've travelled life's long way.

*Kath Finney*

## CHARIOT OF FIRE

I wanted Lollobrigida,
I wanted Betty Grable,
I wanted Bardot or Monroe,
I ended up with the Mabel!

Mabel wanted Cary Grant,
Or Brando, or Bruce Lee,
Or Humph, or Dirk or Errol Flynn,
She ended up with me.

Mabel longed to be a star,
But didn't have the figure,
I longed to be Roy Rogers, but
I didn't have a Trigger.

I would have liked to be Dad,
And Mabel be a mother,
A Gina and a Marlon, say,
And not just one another.

Heigh-ho, instead we travel far,
We search for films, and see 'em,
In Capitol, and Odeon,
And Ritz, and Coliseum.

For in our streetcar named Desire,
(Our little van, a Bedford)
Mabel is my Meryl Streep,
And I'm her Robert Redford!

*Peter Davies*

## WHAT HAVE YOU DONE WITH ALL MY POEMS . . .?

What have you done with all my poems?
Do you read them on occasion . . .
When a full moon turns your mind
To fantasy . . . and find
I'm there . . . embellished in your heart!
You'll not escape me easily . . .
We loved too deeply
And drank too much of nature's cup . . .
But that was long ago -
A careless love . . . but even so,
A ransom could not buy release -
Our poetry now is all we have
To heal our self-inflicted wounds . . .!
So what have you done with all my poems?
Treasure them, my love . . .
Treasure them forever!

*Russell Humphrey*


## THE PATCHED SLEEVE

She found an old coat in her wardrobe
And reached in, to throw it away.
When suddenly, there in her mind's eye,
She pictured a bright summer's day.

The coat was the colour of sunshine,
Out-dated, as some fashions go,
And a tear in the sleeve had been mended,
So neatly, as hardly to show.

Yes, the weather was perfect that summer,
Remembering now, made her smile,
How her sleeve became caught on the barbed wire,
As he lifted her over the style.

Was it really the barbed wire that tore it?
Or could it have been Cupid's dart.
But she smiled, as she tenderly fingered
The place where she'd once worn her heart.

*Hilda Jones*


## TO MY LOVE

The trees wore leaves of green
The day I first met you
And before they turned to brown
I knew my love was true

Like a dream you came to me
So handsome and so tall
Your hair as black as a raven's wing
To you I gave my all

I gave my life to share with you
A life of happiness and bliss
You promised to be true to me
And we sealed that promise with a kiss

It's ten years since first we met
You've love me tenderly and true
You've held me close and made me glad
When I've felt low and sad

You've given all that you could give
And asked nothing in return
Except my love which I shall give
Darling as long as we two shall live

*Hazel F Smith*

## SONNET TO A DARK-EYED GIRL

In The Red Fox Bar on the Ring of Kerry,
Irish folk songs with a rock-n-roll beat.
Young and old were making merry,
Elderly crofters, tapping their feet.
And a friendly, dimpled, dark-haired girl
Showed me her petticoat and a glimpse of knee.
She showed her petticoat with a jig and a twirl
And her dark brown eyes took advantage of me.
With dimpled cheeks and a flashing smile
Put a hand to her hair, and tossed a curl.
I took her waist and we danced for a while,
Gyrating as one in a jiving swirl.
Her moistened lips held their bright red smile
And I fell in love with the dark-eyed girl.

*John Merritt*


## MY SPECIAL LOVE

Like coffee and cream,
Like a favourite dream
Like a sparkling stream
You're special.

Like the team that won
Like the comedian's pun
Like a day in the sun
You're special

Like *a little bit more*
Like winning the draw
Like a waltz 'cross the floor
You're special

38

No-one else can compare
Such perfection is rare
I thank heaven you're there
And are special

*Margaret Myttion*


## VALENTINE'S DAY

I first saw you on Valentine's Day,
And fell in love with you straight-a-way.
There could never be anyone,
To take your place,
The moon and stars shone from your face,
As time passed by,
You loved me too,
With the kind of love,
That grew and grew.

As the years passed by,
We were still together,
I knew this love would last forever,
Then one day you went away,
I knew the time had come for me to say,
I would always love you,
And you could always come back to stay,
What more could a mother say,
To her baby that was born,
On Saint Valentine's Day.

*Muriel Richmond*

## SO CLOSE AND YET SO FAR

It's over forty years now since we first met,
A blind date it was, I do not regret,
And now in the autumn of our years,
Our children have their lives, their worries and cares,
I thought now we would have each other and time to share
Then fate came along and took you from me,
You're now in your own world; where I cannot be,
But through all the bad and the good days,
To me you will always shine bright like the sun's rays.
If God is good and hears my prayers,
Then I will know he really cares,
Together we will be, with love in our hearts,
A second chance of love we can start.
But then we know that God works in mysterious ways,
Who am I to ask for my love to stay
All we can ask is he will be by our side
Giving us strength and love, and with us abide.

*A E Robson*

## HOW DO I KNOW?

When I said 'I love you,'
You asked, 'How do you know?'
By the ache that's in my heart
Each time I see you go.

I know, because I'm lonely
When you are out of sight,
And I long for you to hold me
In the middle of the night.

I know, because I worry
When you're troubled and you're sad.
And when you work too long and hard,
And when I make you mad.

I know, because I think of you
Each minute of the day.
And I feel so happy, when
Sometimes you can stay.

I know because my heart beats fast
Whenever you're around,
And I feel I'm floating
Ten feet above the ground.

I know because my happiest hours
Are when you're here with me.
I know, I love you darling
You're inside me, can't you see?

*Valerie Sparrow*


## A WINDOW TO MY HEART

I only want to hold you
And look into your eyes,
And know that looking back at me
Are eyes that will never lie.

Eyes that say they love me,
And mean *in every sense*,
Eyes that promise happiness
In every glint of lens.

Eyes that understand me,
And want me for who I am.
Eyes that will never hurt me,
And will always give a damn.

I think you have those eyes my love,
To protect and cherish me,
You have my eyes, my heart, my soul,
For everyone to see.

*Victoria L Williams*

## TO ROGER

We fell in love
Then we were wed
How the time
Has quickly fled

Thank you for
The times together
Even through
The stormy weather

We've had six children
Three boys, three girls
Some with straight hair
Some with curls

Three of them
Now have families too
Making us proud grandparents
of six - phew!

It might have been
A struggle at times
But with God's help
We've got through the grime

God taught us how
To grow in love
When needing help
To seek Him above

So thank you for
Those wonderful years
We've spent together
Without too many tears

So bless us Lord
Our marriage to keep
Without too many worries
And losing too much sleep

Amen

*Pam Thompson*


## SUMMER

All night my clamorous pain
subsides against you.
You hold me to your hollows
steeped in sleep.
A liquid bonding begins,

the essence of me
flows into you.
In the air between us
a sweet candour
a melting substance.

Ever since that night -
a new growth inside me.
A tender urgency
like the ripening in dark plums
in the garden.

Tangy flesh of summer
falling,
from time to time
softly -
ready.

*Tricia Corob*

## FOR NIKKI

Enfolded in your summery warmth.
Wrapped up in a tender blanket.
You must have felt my heart beat next to yours like a caged
Bird fluttering in my chest.

My shirt carried your sweet perfume.
My memory carried the brief silk of your lips.
I could have held you all day, held the world at bay.
You make me feel strong and weak all at once.

Your golden hair tickling my cheek.
Eyes closed there was only you in the world.
For once I couldn't think of anything to say.
My dreams realising themselves - nothing needed said.

*Mike Boyle*


## MARRIAGE

And now at last with my band of gold
Your true love forever to hold
As the days pass into weeks and on -
Our love growing ever strong
The sky is forever blue
Like your love always true
Always in your eyes
With the depth of the ocean deep
And height and breadth of the skies.
Your love ripples across the vastness to my shore
The love of marriage is far more precious than before.
Our love is a vacuum, nothing shatters the silence
Growing like a tree, forever in the sunshine.
A key to the door of life.

***Sue Bonning***

44

## UNTITLED

I hear him calling my name
As I sleep
He calls like a red curve
Through the air

I can't sleep
I call your name

You dream you hear me
Calling your name
And wake
With blood in your mouth

Recognise this
The knife's slice
Stripping the skin
Paring down
Red within red within red
Exposing this strange love poem

*Carol Hodgson*


## A GOLDEN CHRYSALIS

I listened to your heartbeat, embedded in the darkness,
Your blue eyes shone, a beacon in the night,
Softly, whispers travelled on fragile waves of jasmine,
A touch of silk and waking embers light.

Your faint breath instilled, with subtle tones of spearmint,
Alighted on my lips and gently kissed,
My tingling skin teased, by locks of shining chestnut,
And hearts welded eternal, in a golden chrysalis.

*Thomas A Rattray*

# I BELIEVE IN LOVE

Love has a special power that brings people together
If you give love away it's remembered forever
Love is the most precious gift you can give
It's the secret of life the reason we live.

Look to your friends, children, husband or wife
Without this gift there would be no new life
With every passing day in love you must believe
The more you give away the more you'll receive.

*Janet Johnson*

# THE ARRIVAL

Bored bodies block the corridor while others
hold up the walls, in ones and twos,
tedium mizzles down through nicotine air
shrouding us in mid-week torpor, and then -

Incandescence on two short legs
comes wheeling round the corner
head down like a charging bull.
Sporting a heart-stopping look
which he's been practising for years,
he cruises by on an after-shave wave
just zipping through the sea of students
who re-knit in his wake,
as he effects and entry
into O three eight.

*June Handford*

## DAYDREAM

As I look up I see her smiling face again
Beautiful girl of age twenty or so
Who is she, what is she, where is she going to
Where is she living and who does she know?

As she walks nearer I think it is possible
I could go up to her and ask for her name,
Then I see there is a partner to follow her,
So I turn around and my life stays the same.

*Clive McCarthy*


## FIRST LOVE

Cupid's arrow travelled straight -
A fleeting silver dart,
It flew until it rested
In my unsuspecting heart.

There was no warning
of its haste,
Just overwhelming passion,
at an unexpected pace.

Can this be true,
this feeling so divine?
Setting pulses racing
as I float upon cloud nine.

Warmth floods my soul
as I nestle in your arms -
A very willing victim
of dear Cupid's charms.

*Elizabeth Robertson*

## IOANNA ATHENE

Athene oh Athene in all that you may
Bring unto this Paris warmth love and stay
Within my sunny days moonlit nights
All unto lover's charms embracing arms
Nights entwined spent sweet wine of love
In dancing Samba oh my dear sabre
Lingering sweet warm wet scabbard

Drifting into my mind's eternal sky
If only you know'st that you fly
In all dreams nightly unto me
Feeling sensuous love within my breath
As imprison in our tower of love
Athene hands touching who
Be my warmth and beauty too

Athene oh Atehene does thou not see'st
In this Paris all love unto you dear'st
As kissing your sweet lips I seek
be my Athene in nightly moods
As Paris brings all his earthly love
Unto this maiden whom is miss
My days longing just for a kiss

From the beauty as is told
Unto Athene can I be so bold
As this poet but bares his soul
These words fly from within
By my arrow straight and true
Flying flying seeks your loving heart
But Paris how do I start

*Edward Ward*

## LOST LOVE

You've gone, my love,
And living now can never be the same,
Your gentle arms are here no more
To soothe away the pain.
We had our plans for future years,
To live and love together,
But now these hopes and dreams are gone -
I'll miss you dear, for ever!
Now my life is sad and lonely,
And my thoughts oft' lead to tears -
But I still recall the love we shared
Through all those happy years.
For nearly forty years we both,
In health and sickness too,
Shared our sorrows and our joys
And thought we'd make it through.
But it was not to be, my love -
Now it's not *us* but only *me*,
For the power that rules our lives decreed
You could not stay with me.

*Freda Rogers*


## MY FAVOURITE HIM

He stroked my hair and kissed me
And soothed me with his voice
As kind and warming as the sun
I really had no choice.

This was the man, the one for me
There could never be another
Me for him, and him for me
Husband, friend and lover.

*Heather H Dawson*

## MY DEAR HUSBAND

A party - how exciting, will you come at 9.02,
The invitation stated Orchard Place, there houses few,
A farewell to three friends, well known, a sad but happy day,
For I can maybe visit them in countries far away.

The thought of what to wear took days of shopping just for shoes,
The dress was green and flowing, the neck low cut and new,
The stockings thin and feminine, stilettos all the rage,
Hair coiffeured, make-up - hours for each - I'm ready for the stage!

The guests arrived, I knew a few but most were strangers all
And there across the room I spied young, handsome, broad and tall,
'Have you met Colin, friend of John's?' the introduction said,
We then sat down and chatted, no inkling where it lead.

Five hundred miles apart were we, 'Come to my home' I asked,
And there we met, two precious days, a bond was made to last.
A posting overseas came soon, so in the days we had
We looked and felt, and talked and shared, good times and yet sad.

For eighteen months, while overseas, letters took the place
Of loving hands, yes, writer's cramp, but ne'er a warm embrace,
But love, so much we learned of each, in writing from the heart
We knew each other, found the source and managed though apart.

Now thirty years have flow by with our mem'ries, joyful thanks
For children, four girls of the best, not money in the bank!
They bring to us such happy times, could we have asked for more?
My loved one, he is still around, loved, hugged and yes - adored!

*Elizabeth M Sudder*

## HE'S MY EVERYTHING

He's the crystal in every raindrop
that cascades from the skies.
He's the sapphire in the oceans and the seas.
He's the gold within the sunshine
that brightly shines above.
He's the emerald in the grass, the leaves and trees.

He's the diamond in the heavenly stars
studded in the night time skies.
He's the ruby in the deepest reddest rose.
He's the topaz in the cornfields
landscaped across the dales.
He's the beauty and the sparkle in our lives.

He's the gemstone in each flower bed
clustered in its fragrance sweet.
He's the precious stone that never ceases shining.
He's the opal in each heavenly cloud
that drifts within the skies.
He's the silver that's revealed within the lining.

He's the jewel within the rainbow
that glistens through the rain.
He's the amethyst that's used in works of art.
He's the Son of God called Jesus
who shed his precious blood.
He's the cultivated pearl within my heart.

What is money! What are values!
When God's given us so much.
We are rich so very rich beyond all measure.
We've the finest master craftsman
to refine for us our lives.
Let Jesus be your priceless daily treasure.

### *Teressa Rhoden*

## THERE YOU WERE

When I came back - there you were -
Still waiting for me,
There you were at the station
As the train steamed in,
I leant out of the window
And I couldn't believe it -
After all this time, year on year,
I couldn't believe it - there you were.

We were a sorry lot back from the camps,
Back from the Japanese jungle,
Minus an arm, minus a leg,
With haunted eyes of bad memories,
Fevered faces,  and spare ribs,
None of us believed there would be anyone
To meet us, to greet us, to care,
But as the train stopped - there you were.

After all the years between us
You were the same, your eyes, your hair,
Your wide warm smile didn't falter
Yet the wreck I must have looked,
But you only had eyes for my love,
The love to which I'd held fast,
Searching to find if it was still there,
And there you were waiting - there you were.

*Esme Francis*

## MY VALENTINE

How glamorous they seemed to be, with
Romantic verse for all to see.
Victorian charm, with rose, red hue,
Edged with lace, and scented too.
Some with romantic verse inside,
To get one of those, I would have died.

I watched the postman coming near,
Hoping he was coming here.
All my friends, with beaming smiles
Clutching cards that travelled miles.
All with their message, Oh, so clear,
Be my Valentine, darling, dear.

Then one fine day, he turned the gate,
And I had my first, it was my fate.
I opened it with trembling hand
To see who had sent it, over land,
From where, from whom, I could not see.
Or even think, who could love me.

I searched the message hid within,
My head was in an awful spin.
But though I tried to read the name,
With bated breath and all aflame.
Though I perused but every line.
I *never* found my Valentine.

***Gwyneth Pritchard***

## SHADES OF PURPLE

Pale Violet in a lilac shade
Gardens on within her fragrant glade
Looking down on sunny forty two
Don on their rip roaring barbecue
Peeks a Poppy shrieks kisses and tells
And leads a congo line through old bluebells.

The brambling lovers stained as dark as wine
Ignore her as they tangle in the vine
The blushing lovers braving Truth and Dare
Don't seem to spy shy Violet clinging there
With wild rose and clematis to the wall
As briars snatch at her to make her fall

She staggers up but falls back with a moan
And Hyacinth leaves a message on her phone
'Miss you petal. Running late.'
He disconnects and leaves her to her fate.
The blues wail up from patios below
And shadows slope down, mauve and indigo.

Pale Violet by dark night's shade
Chokes and faints within her glade
Poison words in a sweet voice she hears
Justifying all her secret fears
'Poppy petal, my true love I vow!
Violet and I are ancient history now.'

Two lovers strolling in the lavender grass
Brush against hidden Violet as they pass
Violet bites her dusky tongue and gnaws magenta berries
Inky Briony she chews and sips at sloe blue cherries
Swallows bitter agate seeds from purple foxgloves tall
Shuts her shining eyes and turns her face towards the wall.

*Rosaleen Orr*

## UNTIL WE MEET AGAIN

I was called to the hospital late at night
As my brother had died, he had given up the fight.
And seeing him peacefully lying there,
I sadly said a silent prayer.
All the suffering had gone from his dear face,
I thought 'Now he's gone to a happier place'.
At the ripe old age of eighty-seven,
He was sure of a special place in Heaven.
A musician was he, the church organ he played.
And in God's house he worshipped and prayed.
So many choir boys he had trained
All through the years the friendship remained.
Some of those lads, now seventy years old,
Recall their youth and the stories unfold.
One wrote that my brother paved the way
Of life, by example, day by day.
He spoke of his courtesy to the public in general,
To bus drivers, shop-keepers, his concern was exceptional
This was just one of the tributes received,
Which helped me so much at the time that I grieved.
Well, I am so proud that he was my brother,
Whom, never would I have changed for another.
For a brother so thoughtful, so generous and kind,
Would be extremely hard to find.
So I thank God for those precious years
Of love and companionship, laughter and tears.
For I have so many memories to treasure
Of happy times and joy beyond measure.
God bless you, dear brother, I loved you so dearly.
This comes from the heart and I mean it sincerely.

*Norah Carter*

## TO FALL IN LOVE

Each time we meet,
I fall in love, for the first time.
Each caress,
Is like the first time I've ever felt your fingers touch my skin.
Each kiss,
awakens a new sensation.
Each look,
only makes me want you more.
Each breath, against my ear,
makes the passion wash over me,
like a tidal wave, swallowing everything in its path.
I cannot think of anything but this moment.
My anticipation,
then consummation and confirmation of all I feel.
Each smile,
tells me that everything's OK.
And the memory keeps me warm,
when you're away.

*Lynn Michelle Hiller*


## ALWAYS

Your smile is like a ray of sunshine
Your lips so gentle as they touch mine
You still make my heart skip a beat
With those clear blue eyes my knees go weak.
That boyish face still makes me smile
You make my life so worthwhile
Your touch is like a velvet glove
So filled with feeling and true love
Without you Dave, I'd have no life
So glad I am to be your wife
Forever it will last your love and mine
I love you dearly, Valentine.

*Trudy Carpenter*

## ODYSSEY

I struggled down life's mysterious path
Never knowing where it would lead
In torment, pain, fear and wrath
I travelled on
With needs of love and joy
Sometimes to appear
To make the journey easy
To make it crystal clear
That with an open heart and mind
I'd carry on to find
A never ending spiral of good -
Not bad
To make me glad
That I can give what's in my heart
Share my hopes
My dreams
My love
And be thankful I'm alive.

*Sheila Munn*


## LOVE HAPPY LOVE

Love Happy Love
Spirits are young
Not a love song
Left unsung
Days are golden
Nights are long
She dons her kimono
Like Suzie Wong
As she sings . . .
That old  sweet song.

*Rita Kelly*

## ALZHEIMER'S

When I hold your hands,
I see the ravages of time.
Gone, the grace of youth,
When it was in its prime.

Where now, passion's touch,
Or its urgent need.
The loving caress, to follow
Where another's hand would lead.

The light of life has gone.
Destroyed by unkind fate.
And empty eyes
Show, purpose now, is late.

The power of thought,
Like grist unto the mill,
Is shapeless dust
Deprived of form or will.

Is familiarity the bridge
'twixt what has been,
And does it linger still,
Yet, is no longer seen?

So, as I now touch your hand,
I pray that you're still there,
For I would have you know
That I still love and care.

*Florence Barnard*

## MY LOVE FOR YOU

You ask, how, I love you:
I'll tell you, my love -
It's as vast as the stairway,
to heaven above:
As endless and deep,
as the turbulent sea;
and fierce like a storm,
with its intensity.

The warmth of my love;
is in each soft caress;
and I constantly strive,
to bring you happiness:
you're in my thoughts, always;
and when you're not here,
I note, countless moments
'til your footsteps are near.

Body and soul;
I'm committed to you:
What more can I offer?
What else, can I do?
Tell me, dear heart;
is it true love, I see?
I pray, you'll say 'Yes!'
Now, and eternally.

*Patricia Mary Gross*

## SUMMERTIME THANKS

What a lovely day we've had today, and what joy we've had together.
It all began at the break of day; I awoke to summer weather.
At five o'clock, when all sleep had gone, my eyes I opened, first to see
Through the windows gleaming, the bright sun; you'd left the curtains

back for me.

The later you woke, refreshed, from sleep, I heard your laugh and cheery call
And with smiling face you came to peep. Day's begun; you offer your all.
Then it's breakfast time, and so you ask: 'Will it be in or out today?'
'It's out!' I say. So begins our task, making sure I'm fit for the day.

Together we bathe my aching bones, working gently till all is done.
Then out of bed, on my four wheeled throne, ready now to bask in the sun.
Breakfast was good in the wall shadow. Then we strolled among our flowers,
Paths wide enough for my chair to go; soaking up the summer hours.

Afternoon tea in the dappled shade, sitting under the old ash tree,
Where the smell of the lavender made my heart leap and my soul feel free.
The scent of the pinks caressed my skin, above, swallows swooped together,
Bees searched for pollen in the lupin; we're so lucky with this summer!

When the sky was a deep midnight blue and all the birds had gone to bed,
When the task of my bedtime was through and all the papers we had read,
God I thanked for all you do and say, blessed Him for the summer weather,
And thought: 'What a lovely day today and what joy we've had together.'

*Sheila E Harvey*

## FIRST LOVE

Beneath the clock at half past two
My love and I did meet,
How young were we, and so in love,
Flowers bloomed about our feet
Or so we thought, on that far off day
When we met in Market Street.

We wandered round the market pens,
High with the heat of day,
But all we smelled was the lilac flower
And the scent of new mown hay
And that freshly delicate, new born smell
Of the rose that blooms in May.

Cream buns we ate in the pastry shop
Were served right royally,
With all the nectar of the gods
In that cracked brown pot of tea.
And the moon shone right down Market Street
When she said goodbye to me.

We have lived long years and have loved again,
Since we wandered in dust and flowers,
I have been where despair begins,
She has dwelt in ivory towers,
But 'til life has gone or the world is old,
That day will still be ours.

*A Florence Otterburn*

## POPPIES

If I could tell the world about you,
They'd only wonder how
I manage to go on living without you,
But you're still in my heart, even now.

I still remember those summer days,
And those wonderful summer nights.
The poppies shimmering in the haze,
And those twinkling Heavenly lights.

Sometimes we'd just lie close and still,
Not a syllable passing between us,
I loved you then, and always will.
As beautiful as Venus.

Or embraced in each others arms so tight,
That scarcely could we breathe.
And never did I want to fight,
That wonderful spell you'd weave.

Your eyes were the lure that captured me,
Out-shining your golden bangles.
Then the whole of you enraptured me.
And for a time, I walked with angels.

*J H Woolfries*


## IF I LOVED YOU ANYMORE

If I loved you anymore
My surroundings I would not see
For my blindness would effect
The land and beauty percepted by me.

If I loved you anymore
Than I do today
My body would explode
For such intensity of feelings
Will never ever go away.

If I loved you anymore
My mind wouldn't belong to me
You would possess it like my body
Bit by bit, every inch of me, totally.

If I loved you anymore
It's no coincidence, not just lust
I believe my destiny lies within you
My fate, my life's lover, a good man, someone who I can trust
I could not love anybody, anymore!

*Janice Johnson*


## MY LOVE
*(Dedicated to Julie Ann Turner)*

It seems so long ago since I comforted you
The leaves where green, the air was sweet and warm
The moon was bright and giving, the tide rushed in
   True love was born

My love it seems so long ago since I kissed you
The wonder of love was portrayed in our eyes
Reflections give solace to the earth
Can a day like this ever pass us by?

My love is seems so long ago since I give you my heart
In a passionate embrace our love burned
   The world turned
Then the seasons changed they changed

Could it be that I am in love with a dream?

*Francis Farnworth*

## JAN

I did not want Jan to live in immortal lines
But in my heart and, beyond, in my soul
I did not want poetic lines to prosper whilst life sets down
Its load to another less fortunate generation that feels little
And reads more endless words telling of our love.

I wanted Jan to live me and be my love
And watch how every day I love her the most
Knowing day's love is final and never again increasing
Whilst tomorrow's is more, infinite and continual
Until it is today's again, and so never loved more than now before
So, again, more than yesterday, and impossibly, less than tomorrow
Becoming today and so until the end of time.

That Jan, is the love impossible that is ours
Possible as it grows, stops, becomes everything
And then grows again
Like our universe
Ever expanding, never diminishing
Its beginning everlasting with no end possible.

Ours is an impossible love.
Except that it is endless, more-most today's tomorrow and
tomorrow's today
Make it so possible
To love you and be loved by you
Each and every single day, once again, anew.

So I can say over and over again, 'I love you today more than yesterday
And never can I love you more since this is the most felt today.'
Until- that is - tomorrow yet again becomes today and
Today is yesterday loved even more than ever before.

*Faysal Mikdadi*

## FAIR EXCHANGE

Give me your love and I'll give mine
  And never rue the giving;
Such fair exchange I deem divine:
  Shared love is highest living.

Grant me the fortune of your smile,
  And favour me with kisses,
So that for a blissful while
  My heart exults in riches.

Tell me the treasure of your choice
  And conquer me with daring,
The classic song of love's own voice
  To bardic gems comparing.

The crowning virtue of your ways
  I'll garland all with gladness:
A coronet of silvern praise
  To banish winter's sadness.

No shadow e'er fall between us!
  No captious word of cold change
Breathe doubting cloud upon us -
  Constant shines love's fair exchange!

Give me your love; in love we'll grow,
  In ceaseless splendour sharing.
Who knows more than true lovers know?:
  Wise love is equal caring.

*Leslie E Thomas*

## TOKEN

I may not always tell you
But you really are the best.
I often get emotional
When you're standing in your vest.

I love the way your eyes shine
And glisten, all white and red.
And I love the way your dandruff sits
So snugly on your head.

I love to see you slumber
When you're sitting in the chair.
And the way you sometimes chatter
Even when there's no one there.

I love it when your teeth clatter
As you dribble in your tea.
And I remember how last birthday
You brushed them just for me.

A hundred touching things you do
All make me love you more.
And no matter what the doctor says
You're not always a bore.

So darling, please forgive me
If at time I may upset you.
Like the swarm of flies that follow you
I never can forget you.

*Janice Fixter*

## SOUL PROVIDER

Seconds spanning years we have been together through times both
thick and thin. We had our share of weeping.
Sometimes our downs outweighed the ups and in your arms I cried
myself to sleep. Finding shelter in your keeping.

How I ache to show you that I care whenever you feel low I want
to share. A funny tale, a rhyme, a joke.
Anything to bring a smile to the one who nurtures my love with
gentle guiding hands. So fragile the unseen yoke.

You held on to my heart and soul so tightly when I raved and
fretted to be freed. Impassioned by some foolish creed.
You let me keep my space and my dreams even when you didn't
understand a thing. Smiling as you laughingly agreed.

Yet as the sun shelters the moon we stayed arm in arm, heart to
heart, and soul to soul. Facing the passages of time.
I knew that your strength was bolder, braver than mine, and as
long as we stand united. The whole world is mine.

*Marjorie Finney*


## LOVE'S ENCOUNTER

Softly run your fingers through my hair
You are a sunbeam hard to catch - and fair,
You live another life away from me,
And your eyes beg me to let you stay - free.

Beautiful and tender is your hand,
You ask me to be strong, to understand,
But I have nothing to replace
Your company, and gentle face,
Don't leave me yet!
We've only just met!
How swift is time
To end my rhyme.

*Vera Torbet*

## THREADS OF LOVE

It's alright I know the way to go.
Sometimes the track may be dusty with no open road,
The bushes may grow high and be saddled with thorns;
But the comparison is small when the alternative is that of a
         mother's needle sharp scorn.
For as she sits embroidering her age-torn cloth
Piercing my character and urging you to stop,
Remember this bond, the colour of our thread,
It thrives and is alive; not frayed and dead.
You have to trust me as we travel this track,
As once you've sewn your heart on your sleeve there's no going back,
For love cannot be ruled by brittle words of steel,
But by the finery of life it takes form and becomes real.
I may not be rich but hold the tapestry of life,
With love our cloak; our protector from strife.
Just as your mother catches her finger and bleeds onto cloth;
Flesh will recover and heal but the stain will reveal the cost.

*Kirsty Steer*


## LOVE CONQUERS ALL

When the long, long, line of life cannot extend,
O'er the mantle of our days that have to end,
And the physic of our lives becomes resigned,
In the distant dark a light comes to remind,
That I have thought of nothing else but thee!

When the shape of land that goes from pole to pole,
Is by nature changed to court a different role,
A broad echo keeps resounding in my head,
Of thy voice and all the things thou ever said,
And I can think of nothing else but thee!

When the sun expires and splinters into ash,
And the moon and stars begin to fall and crash,
The whole wide world convulses into spin,
Through the turmoil hear me shout above the din,
That, with all my heart and soul, I love thee!

When the universe becomes a mass that is no more,
And future lays itself in wait beside death's door,
God in his sanctum breathes his very last,
As man finally is conquered by the blast,
But our love can never die, and we live on!

*Stan Mason*


## THE FADED ROSE

The faded rose stands in the corner now,
in a special place,
I look at it from time to time
as the light brings out its beauty.
Each waxen petal standing proudly,
I watch,
as they unfold their crushed velvet layers
to be brushed by the amber mists
of the sun-laden rays.
I remember when you handed me
this scarlet bud of memory
in another special place,
when the light filled the room
and the perfume touched our hearts.

*Bettina Jones*

## HUSBAND

Husband what a nice name it really
        sounds so grand,
but to know the meaning is hard to understand,
        but as the years they pass you by it's
then you understand that
H is for the help he gives to you
U for understanding
S for sympathy
B for the best he sees in you and
        all his love's there too
A for another year that's gone
N for never apart
D for the dearest in your heart
        which makes him your sweetheart
Put all the letters together and you
        will see they spell
The name I've called my poem
        *Husband!*

*Isabel Platt*


## A WALK WITH MARY

A walk we could afford those wartime days;
Young lady and boy,
Down the High Street and the country by-ways;
Quite naive and coy.

So many times I can still remember
Walking hand in hand;
In the warm summer or in December,
Many years they've spanned.

All life's roadways we have walked together;
The high and the low;
In much sunshine but some stormy weather,
For thus the years go.

Yes, strolling hand in hand for fifty years -
Sweethearts, man and wife -
Not forgotten, but forgiven, the tears,
Now gone any strife.

Those treasured walks soon after we were wed -
By the river banks -
For such pleasures as life still goes ahead,
We humbly give thanks.

The giving of thanks is no platitude -
No foolish blether -
This we have done - for which our gratitude -
Walked life together.

*Roy Hammond*


## STIRRING OLD ROOTS

Your hand touching my hair revives spring-times
Uncertainties. Shyness remembered, not
Really felt, a surface wakening only;
Less than the memory of a waking dream.
Like an old battery that flickers still
Without illumination; or a bulb
That brightens as it dies.
     But always,
Too deep within me to be touched by you
Or anyone, wrapped in a worn-out mantle
Of indifference, the lark still rises
On a summer hill and love still laughs there
In the meadowlands, where we were young once
Many years ago, that I can reach yet.
Too far for you to follow even when
Caressing hands touch springtime roots with pain.

*Dorothy Davis-Sellick*

## THERE'S LOVELY

I'm sorry I don't speak Welsh
I'm mothered Welsh but
she gave it up for bread
and an English roof above her head

Dew you're so right I never had the Welsh
I diolck yn fawr and I guess nos da
but I really don't know Welsh

I understand a little 'Thomas', there's posh
but that will never, never wash
I think Welsh
I breathe Welsh
I walk Welsh
I sing Welsh in my head
I eat Welsh
I drink Welsh
I see Welsh
I touch Welsh in my bed
I love Welsh
I hear Welsh
I trust Welsh
I know Welsh I am led

Still you're right I only speak '*next door*'
There's pity when all's done and said
perhaps I'd make my feelings clearer
with a Welsh tongue in my head.

*Judd Hulme*

## A HANDFUL OF ROSE PETALS

When you are old my darling, or weary and alone,
when letters go unanswered and no friends telephone,
do not despair my darling, no need to feel so weak,
you have this book of messages, wherein warm love may speak
of crystal tinted moments, of jewelled minutes caught
within the hand of friendship, when times were ne'er so fraught
as those that you imagined. Here, captured in a phrase,
long may each sweet thought tremble, surrendering its praise.

These were the fragrant moments when roses came to bloom,
and, even when as petals, I caught them for my loom,
these words should not embarrass you, nor shame your hours of ease:
they sing of happy notions, they rarely aim to tease.
'Tis how I share for ever the dewdrop on the stem
and plant along your pathway the double sided gem
of variable responses, of smiles and lost embrace,
of wondrous sudden pauses, of laughter in your face,
of comforting caresses, the secret gentle touch,
the times when you imagined I suffered overmuch.

And if you will, my darling, cannot the time recall,
which in these darkling phrases I pen for you, my pall
shall be this book of verses. Poor happy, happy fool
who loved and did endeavour to cultivate this rule:
that beauty lies in loving, that truth shall be confessed.
Whate'er the price of loving, in payment I am blessed.
And you in idle moments may take this book and read
how once you were enchanting someone who felt your need.

*George Pearson*

## IN RETROSPECT AND DREAMS . . .

Between my daughters visits
I have time to smile down on the years.
In retrospect, I feel I've been truly blessed
To have seen the wondrous awakening
Of my daughters youth, into the maturity of fulfilment.

I know two parts have combined
Breaking the fragile shell of innocence
To form a perfect whole.
You have now spread your wings
To new horizons, to tread the distant
Alien soil, and taste wine on other lips.

Now my heart burns with sincere devotion
As new life will soon begin from you.
Life like a rainbow being many colours,
And the deep ruby red -
Which will run like a living thread
Throughout your life and through my heart
A body sweetly laced with honey
That I shall hold tightly to my breast
Close in bonds of love.

*Ann-Marie Lofkin*


## HOLDING SOMEONE NEW

Just one look from her glowing eyes
Can paint out all the darkness in my skies
And just one smile from her painted lips
Could sink my heart like a thousand ships

I never thought I'd love again
Always been to hell and back and then
I met you, cold December night
And all my past wrongs became a right

Sometimes we never give a chance
So blinded by our pasts to see romance
When commitments break our hearts in two
We shy away from holding someone new

When I saw you standing at my door
I searched my soul and could not wish for more
In the midst of cold and darkened night
February's future seemed so bright

Then she left and I could see
Just how vulnerable hearts can be
She made me laugh, she helped me smile
But will I have the chance to make her mine.

*Lee Nelson*


## MY MAN

Alright so you are elderly, you still possess the charm,
Which drew me many years ago into your loving arms.
Your hair and beard are silver, your cheeks are rosy red.
Your brown eyes still can twinkle at cheeky things you've said.
Your figure now is plumper, more stately is your walk,
Your brain is still as active that's never been at fault.
The music that you play me comes straight from up above.
When you sit at your console to perform with so much love.
From day that I first met you plus all the ones between.
I only have to see you to feel again sixteen.
We may live on a pension, money therefore tight.
As long as you are with me I know my world's alright.

*Barbara Goode*

## NATASHA

A glance across a packed out bar,
Straight to your eyes that seemed so far,
Lonely looks, yet surrounded by a crowd,
It all seems quiet but everything's loud.

I speak to you first and then you reply,
It's easy to see that we're both quite shy,
We stammer and stutter and make a chat,
A lovely memory to look back at.

Next time we meet, we're all on our own,
A nice evening out and I walk you home,
Our lips go together and then pull away,
Should I go home or should I stay.

We kiss again in the warm Summer's night,
Even now it all seems right,
Just one more kiss - if I may,
And then we turn and walk away.

We sit down and think, it's easy to know,
That this new love is going to grow,
My meeting with you is like finding a treasure,
I want to be with you forever and ever.

*A Preston*


## NOTHING TO DO

there is nothing to say but
I love you
there is nothing to think
but thoughts of you
of loving you

nothing else remains
nothing else sustains

76

all else is but a diversion
everything else a poor relation

when I am away from you
my mind is a one way track
back to you
and I find I can't wait
to be there with you
be near you

where there is nothing to do
but love you

*Fiona Clark*


## A PROMISE

He comes to me with sunlight in his eyes
And the smile he gives shows no surprise
To feel his hand upon my face
To me there is no better grace

His fingers running through my hair
Oh how many times have I longed to be there
He speaks his voice is quiet and low
Words heavy with meaning but how can he know

Longing and waiting, wanting only to be near
Is it only in my dreams that I ever come here
How can I tell him he's captured my heart
But he's promised me now we never shall part

I am him and he is me
What stronger love could there be
A look that takes away the tears
To be carried with me through the years
promises made beneath the skies
And he comes to me with sunlight in his eyes

*Amanda Everatt*

## I LOVE YOU

'I love you'
My heart sings to the world
And the breeze
On his way,
Carries my words
To the trees
And the leaves whisper
'I love you.'

'I love you'
The voice of the sea, as he turns in his tide
And the waves
Splash the shore,
Breaks forth in song
With me
And carries my message
'I love you'

'I love you'
And to you it comes
On the wind
And the sea
And I wait and listen
For maybe
They will return with a message for me
'I love you.'

*Mary Cox*

## AN EVERLASTING LOVE

Your bright blue eyes sparkle in your smile.
With you I'd walk an everlasting mile.
My love for you will always be.
Never ending, lasting, wild and free.

Your tenderness, your caring, your love
I hold dear.
My heart beats fast when you are
Near.
I love you more each passing day
I know our love is here to stay.

Your touch is warm, your smile sincere
I hold you close when you are here.
I've loved you since I love you still
And my love I always will.

The day we met I always knew
One day I would love you
I love you more than you will know
My love for you will always grow.

When I am sad and feeling blue
I know I can always turn to you
You have made my life so worthwhile
Now I am happy, now I can smile.

I'll treasure you my whole life through
Until the end of time I'll love you
You mean more to me than I can say
I know our love will always stay

*Sharon Andrews*

## HE'S GONE

With us you could have kept in touch
How could you hurt us both so much
A letter, a ring or even a call
Wouldn't have been much effort at all

Our love and hearts from us you did steal
Why did you leave us knowing how we would feel
Up until now our friendship you've shared
For us we thought you loved and you cared

To say goodbye was the least you could do
It's been such a long time since first we met you
Our love and our friendship to you we did hand
But now at least we know where we stand

*Christine Brooks*


## MY KIND OF HEAVEN

If I could live my life again
Not one moment would I rue
Again once more I'd like to share
My heaven on earth with you
I think of all the happy days
We always spent together
And never really had to care
Through fine or stormy weather
You once said how lovely it was to love
But to be loved was lovelier still
You filled my life with happiness
For nothing more could I wish
But to hope that many others
Will share such wedded bliss.

*Margaret Blackwell*

# TINY BEJEWELLED BUTTERFLY THING

Once upon a time there was a tiny bejewelled butterfly thing
All diamond sparkly, bursting with rainbow light
A bright darting sunbeam, oh so anxious to sing
Waiting in the wings - poised to brighten someone's plight.

Enter lonely kingfisher charged full of pride - but oh so sad
Nature's flying kaleidoscope of coloured perfection
Desperate to fly here, there - anywhere; glad
To move on; aimless existence - the epitome of dejection.

*'Why so sad?'* Butterfly thing landed on kingfisher's head
A tiny multicoloured aeroplane ready, dying to please
*'I'm sad, no-one to share things with'* he said
The better to study him she moved her position with ease.

Interested now he ceased his hunt for dragonfly
And gave the rainbow aeroplane his full attention
*'It's like this I need love'* his beautiful eyes were far from dry
*'Perhaps you'll be my loving friend?'* he heard himself mention.

Why creep in the shade if you can walk  tall in the sun?
His thought spoke volumes as he studied his friend
Could this ever be the happiness after all I have won?
She read his mind - life with him I can certainly commend!

Fantasia, wonderment and all that's good
Shone in their faces as they savoured this new perfection
Reaching out to the other for Spiritual food
We're in love, we're in love - no more loneliness or fear of rejection

*Paul Harvey Jackson*

## ANGEL'S EYES

Angel's eyes look down on me
And lift the veil of mystery
Releasing flocks of pure, white doves
Explaining why I fall in love.

Amidst the mists of feelings deep
I rise from shallow, dappled sleep
To see the vision of my dreams
Unfold in beauteous, silken seas

Her hair is black, and sleek as night
Her face a picture, gleaming bright
Her lips, slight parted, breathing slow
Her countenance, a heavenly glow

Her smile, a lifetime's happiness
Her laugh, a gift, my ears to bless
Her figure, sensuous, lithe and neat
Her walk, so passionate, complete

I reach to hold her fingers long
Electric touch, my heart's in song
My life ignite, my love bursts through
For in my soul, I see it's you

*Phil Sanders*

## KISSING YOU

What is it you do to me?
You send a silver sparkle
Flash of lightning
And sunshine shivers
Through and through
And through me!

*Hev Woodhouse*

## OLD LOVE

Our hands touched I held on seeking
Would this be our last meeting
You let your hands caress the length of mine
The squeeze you give to my finger tips
Before you let them go I knew you were still mine
Only you and I knew of days so long ago
When we held each other sought each other's lips
The eagerness we felt in those young days
In that crowded room only you and I knew
Pleasantries exchanged the moments flew
You turned I knew you must depart
The way you looked you left me your heart
My love of long ago are still mine
In that crowded room of this you give no sign
How many years will I wait to see you again
Left alone I stand with heart so full of pain.

*Edward Inkpen*


## RECOGNITION

I glanced across
you came into view
in that split second
I surely knew
our paths would cross
You'd be mine
our love would stand
the test of time
and all our dreams
will reach fruition
from that first spark
of Recognition.

*Sandra Noyes*

## MY MAN

He would insist on marrying me,
Although I told him then,
That fairly soon I could collapse
And never walk again.
He was such a macho man
I didn't think it fair
To risk saddling him with babies
And a wife in a wheelchair.
He gave me love and comfort
Whilst our child was being born,
And now he lifts me in and out of bed
Each night and morn.
It's true what granny told me,
She knew what she was about.
'Don't marry a man you *could* live with,
Pick the one you just *can't live without!*'

*Pip Phillips*


## TO HAVE LOVED

How I love thee
To the very depths of my soul
What is to become of me?
Love-love me my dearest
Take me wherever
To the dreams of the unknown
Drown me in your sorrows
With every blowing bubble
So that I may live forever.

*Pamela Harrison*

## YOU ARE TRULY AMAZING

You are truly amazing,
there's little else I can say,
the more words that I search for,
the less come walking my way.
All my past frustrations,
all the pain and the tears,
melt away as you hold me
and I forget those lost years.

It was truly amazing,
how from the depths of despair,
I emerged from the ashes
and I found you waiting there.
I'm walking a rainbow,
hand in hand with the sun;
I'm flying higher than high,
true love has finally won.

You are truly amazing,
there has been no other time,
when a love has so touched me,
drowned both my body and mind.
Don't ever stop flowing,
pour down incessantly;
I know without any doubt,
our love will flow endlessly.

*Pauline Ilsley*

## OUR LOVE

If our love should die
I'd try to pretend that I did not care,
Nor would I sigh
And stop to stare
At stranger or friend who reminds me of you
With your golden hair

If our love should die
I'd bury it deep where the hurt can't grow
And try not to cry
Or make any show
Of how, in my sleep, it would torture me
Like a truncheon's blow.

Our love must not die
Or I'd die too and lose all my trust
In God on high,
For surely He must
Know losing you would hurt me as much
As a rapier's thrust.

*Helen Strangwige*


## VALENTINE BABE

I love you for your certain smile
that cheers me when I'm blue
I love you for your gentle ways
that warm me through and through

*Debra Tuck*

## MY HUSBAND

Just how deeply I love you
You would find so hard to believe
But if you ever went away
I know how much I would grieve
Because from the day I met you
I knew that you were the one
For all my hopes and longing
For everyone else had gone
You have brought me happiness
With your tender loving ways
And I know I shall need you
Till the ending of my days
So darling stay beside me
And say you'll leave me never
For as long as I can have your love
I'll be content forever.

*Iris Brown*


## ECSTASY

Ecstasy is to slough off one's tail
as the lizards do,
stretch crumpled wings - from the cocoon -
like a butterfly.

The fuschia flowers pop into bloom
and eschscholtzias drop night-caps
the pomegranate bursts its skin!
Nature's growing is not without pain.

Ecstasy is to find the void
has filled again. The void has given room
to new found hops and jumps and skips.
seeds of hope born out of the gloom.

*Anne Shells*

## IN THE WORLD OF FANTASY

Thank you for your gift, my love
Your insight into reality
Never boring, often intriguing
I admit I was fascinated
With the story
An experience so different
From what lies waiting for me
In my world of fantasy.

But then came craggy cliffs
And bottomless pits
By some cruel twist of fate
A world too harsh and jagged
For me to ever stay
Without the comfort and empathy
That lies waiting for me
In my world of fantasy

Too ethereal for rational explanation
And yet too safe for me to really leave
If the sun, the moon and stars were mine
I'd give them all to you
So that you might somehow
Have a glimpse, my love
At what lies waiting for me
In my world of fantasy

*Emma Sowter*

## ACROSTICALLY YOURS

Always and forever
Love will always be
As lasting as is love itself
No one but you for me.

Always together
Never apart
Deep, deep love, straight from the heart.

Such a love as ours is
Always ever true.
Never failing one another
Do what we might do.
Remember there can only be
A love 'til death parts you and me.

*Alan Potter*


## FOR MARK

Through our generations anger and selfishness
I can feel pleased with my own happiness,
Appreciate all your care,
The fact you are always there,
Willing to share the trivial,
The mundane and the habitual,
Discovering fun in the dullest of things,
Sharing the excitement that family brings,
Actions and words from the heart,
Embracing every part
As lover, joker, father and friend,
Able to reassure, able to brighten,
My optimism and stability;
I am so lucky that you love me.

*Gilly Homan*

## ODE TO MY WIFE

You are my life, my everything
My fragrant blossom in the spring
My radiant glow as the sun above
My one and only everlasting love

The memories that we shared together
Expressed our true love for one another
You stood by me through good and bad
The dearest friend I've ever had

You shower me with love untold
From a heart that's made of purest gold
Thus being with you made me realise
On this earth I've found my paradise

The happiness and joy we often share
Is measured in deeds beyond compare
The blessings from the God above
Bestowed on us everlasting love

When the time has come for us to retire
And we surrender our souls to the supreme power
Then on judgement day when our sins are forgiven
Our eternal love we'll carry into Heaven

*Lawrence Thomas*


## LOST LOVE

You were my joy,
my heaven, my bliss.
Even now, I am
thankful for this.

It was magic for me,
each time that we met.
When I could hold thee,
my eyes were all wet.

Tears for the future?
Then I knew not,
that time would untie
our true lover's knot.

When I could love thee,
my eyes were all bright.
Full of thy beauty,
from morn until night.

Now that I lost thee
were thou ever so dear.
How did I lose thee?
By jealousy and fear.

*Peter Sowter*


## WELL WORN WISH

Love you till
The moon has lost all of its glow
Miss you so
When midnight calls and bedroom
Lights are turned down low.
Your renaissance smile,
Is more precious to me than all the
Worlds silver and gold.
At last!
Someone to love, someone to hold.
I will love you.
Till the sun forgets to shine
I'm so glad cupid
Heard this, my well worn wish, and
He worked extra hard to make you mine.

*Charles Murphy*

## FOLLOW MY HEART

Follow my heart to the one I love,
That's what I must do
Till I find the one I love,
To make my dreams come true
You are the one, I long to kiss
You are the one, I will always miss,
If I had a wish,
It would be for you
To make it come true,
So I will not be sad and blue
Just seeing you, is bliss,
And to marry you
Would be my cherished wish,
Then we could watch,
The stars and moon above,
You are the sweetheart I love

*Joyce Campbell*


## VALENTINE THOUGHTS

We never spoke a word that day but smiles and thoughts can meet,
It seemed we knew each other's mind and did not need to speak.
I'm married to another and she may well be too,
But eyes can flirt much easier than people's bodies ever do.
It was just a fleeting moment, a chance meeting on a bus,
It never could come to be for either one of us.
But thinking's in my make-up - it's better thoughts than deeds,
For actions brings decisions and to problems they must lead.
We'll never meet a second time of that I'm almost sure,
But the moment held more magic than most drugs and tablets cure.

*Paul Sanders*

## INFLUENTIAL LOVE

When songwriters write about Saturday night
as the loneliest night of the week
I quite sympathise with the heart-rending sighs
and their fits of occasional pique
As poets lament over hours they spent
shedding tears when lost love made them blue
I know in my heart they were doomed from the start
for they'd never known one such as you

The love others crave is the kind that you gave
from the very first day our eyes met
Love so precious and rare, it lays the soul bare
never causing one moment's regret
Neither selfish nor mean, just honest and clean,
reliable, tender and true
Supportive and strong if life starts going wrong,
it sustains my resolve to win through

There once was a time things weren't quite so sublime,
when I lived in a turbulent state
Confusion reigned free, feeding rage within me
I though nothing on earth could placate
Now you're at my side, life's a wonderland ride
there's no problem I can't overcome
Though fate's edge may prove keen, you make life serene,
for me, you and nirvana are one.

*Ron Beaumont*

## I'LL BE WAITING

In the spring
on the open road,
I'll be waiting.
In the desert
to take your load,
I'll be waiting.
In a haven
to warm your cold,
I'll be waiting.
By the old log fire
when you grow old,
I'll be waiting.
On Heaven's steps
to meet your soul,
I'll be waiting.

*Alex Southgate  (13)*


## DEDICATION TO GOD, FOR MY MAN

I no longer know what I'm striving for,
I don't see a goal anymore,
At times life seems so unfair,
And of troubles I think, I've had my share.

But due to my love of God and of my John,
I feel the urge to still carry on,
Even through times of harshness and stress,
I struggle along to do my best.

For God made John for me to love,
First down here, then in Heaven above,
And so for me to do right by the two,
There is no pain, anguish or misery I won't go through.

*Linda Smith-Warren*

## FIRST LOVE

I remember - I remember
How we walked through tall green grasses
Hand in hand we faced the sunshine
Silently our hearts were promised.

I remember - I remember
Wading in a sparkling cool stream
Our feet slipping on smooth pebbles
Laughing as we nearly toppled.

I remember - I remember
Standing under the swaying branches
There we said we loved each other
And would love always and ever.

I remember - I remember
Happy times gone and past now
Gone like you away for ever
But in my heart I still remember.

*Norma Peckston*


## VALENTINE

This time in ev'ry year I'm bade to seek a valentine;
But I have none to seek, because I know you're mine.
You've been my valentine for year on passing year
And knowledge of that blesséd state with happiness I wear.

Let's say you'll be my valentine for ever and a day
And that whate'er occurs we'll stay close all the way.
That constant state is all I seek to requite me,
No valentine will e'er be mine that is not surely thee.

*John Pottinger*

## LONDON SPACE

Plane trees that each spring light up London make
Japanese patterns, mostly space:
so airy, so lightly-leaved, they take
your breath away, their first pale April green
scattered on sky or stock brick.
               We two, old
still go our ways about the London house
long years kid-racketed: could have sold
the lease and didn't. Town mouse and mouse,
we warily inhabit the new peace:
and if we aren't habitually at war,
don't, mousing round like whiskered, cease
to value what we couldn't have before,
distance. Spaced, we've scuttled on
companionably: not all have done.

*Pamela Joll*


## WRAP ME IN YOUR ARMS

Wrap me in your arms
Keep me safe, keep me warm,
Take away my fears and destroy them,
Smother me with love.
Wipe away the tears from my eyes
Fill me with happiness.
Take me beyond this world.
And show me Heaven
Take me to your heart and never let me go.
Take away the pain of loneliness
Show me the joy of living
Let me touch the stars and make a wish
To remain here for eternity
Wrapped in your arms

*Pauline Donoghue*

## THOUGHTS

I have so many thoughts of you and of happy days gone by
I have so many dreams of you. I sit alone and sigh
I have so many memories of when our lips were one.
We kissed beneath cold winter's stars and laughed 'neath golden sun.

We loved beneath a yellow moon, the heavens bright above.
We lived in our sweet wonderland vowing our true love.
And now that you are far away and I am filled with pain,
I'll just go on and dream my dreams until we meet again.
I'm filled with deep sad longing, sometimes I gently cry
For I'll always love and cherish you until the day I die.

I'll just go on awaiting, praying every day
That you love me as I love you, true in every way.
I feel so melancholy, lonesome, sad and blue
And the dreams I dream I beg the Lord will make them soon come true.
Then we'll be together always and never have to part
And life with you will be always new my very own sweetheart.

*Fredric Davies*


## MY LOVER COMPARED WITH WATER

Cool me and cleanse me,
Beloved.
Hold me and rock me.
Roll your waves over me.

Let me dive to your depths,
Beloved.
Splash in your shallows,
And rest in your still pools.

Pour me over your steep falls,
Beloved.
Drench me in your flood.
Surround me and fill me.

*Ann Middleton*

## TO MY WIFE

Perchance someone could love thee more,
However, I only know what is at my core.
You are there first, last and always.
Let none be deceived, you are my life,
Love can be painful but no need for strife.
I only know what effect it has on me
So may some feeling be also with thee,

Indeed, sometimes I think all this has to be.

Lovers know what is in each other's mind
Only when these feelings intertwine.
Very soon they become as one,
Every occasion knows it to be so.

You and I wherever we may go,
Over and over we shall have the same words to tell,
Unless and until we're together all will be well.

*Val Gordon*




## YOU'RE PRECIOUS TO ME

If the moon was a pearl
I would take it from the sky
And with a chain of the finest gold
I would lay it before you
Upon a salver of pure silver.

If the stars were diamonds,
Sparkling in the Heavens above,
In all their glory they could not compare,
With the finest diamonds I've ever seen,
Those which sparkle in your eyes.

If the sun was to shine
Forever bright in the sky
Its light could not outshine
The light which shines from you,
O, vision of beauty.

And if the world kept its treasure,
The gold, silver, pearls and diamonds too,
To me there would be nothing more precious,
In this World than you.

*Eric Stevenson*


## EYES FOR YOU

I cannot take
My eyes from you
It is too difficult
For me to do

You are the focus
Of my desire
You burn me up
I am on fire

With the love
I feel for you
So won't you please
Tell me what I must do

For you to return
This deep felt love
I will do it
With help from above.

*Tom Sullivan*

## THE CHERISHING OF DREAMS

I cherish her as I do dreams,
Of moonshine's absent minded beams,
Of growling thunder's faded blast,
Of childhood days of years long past,
    And so it seems,
I cherish her as I do dreams.

I cherish her as I do dreams,
Of shadowed past and future gleams,
Of sunshine in the midst of rain,
Of pleasure in the midst of pain,
    And so it seems,
I cherish her as I do dreams.

    And so it seems,
    And so it seems,
I cherish her as I do dreams.

*James Shillito*


## STRIDER

He strides into my day.
Sharp features grin,
and soft, fine hair falls over eyes
that slide sideways to view,
searchingly.
Warm, flat Yorkshire tones
breathed at me -
soothing,
pleasing,
thrillingly deep -
charm me,
teasing a smile.

*Irena Zientek*

100

## ANGELIC

God loves the creatures that he made
That's why there's heat as well as shade
Fast flowing streams in forest glades
And angels who will masquerade

In human shape and you are one
You shine on me like glowing sun
Or cool me with serenity
By quiet smiles you give to me

When things in life are going bad
You tell me, that you're very sad
Then I prescribe my tenderness
And tell you that you're heaven blessed

Your spirit's on the seventh level
I don't know if there is a devil
But if guns fire and 'copters strafe
I know the Lord will keep you safe

Because I said a special prayer
Now you are always in his care
Untouched by any human force
Except the power of love of course

The earth goes spinning into space
On endless orbits it must chase
If anything could slow it down
The power of lovely eyes of brown

Could almost put it in reverse
Still we can't change the universe
But every time you are with me
The joy I feel is heavenly.

*Philip McLynn*

## ECLIPSE

Though 'twas just a brief eclipse
Of my entire adulation,
Your absence gave abundance
To the sense of deprivation.
My eyes and mind adorned
To thy peace and tranquillity,
Sought restoration of the norm,
The semblance of sanity.

Guilt, born of nothing
Merely residing separate places,
I in a place we'd been together,
Aone, no familiar traces,
Your warm, comforting hand
In its absence more conspicuous,
In love but not with love,
Thy love. . . truly ubiquitous.

*Ashley Goodwin*


## SHALL I?

Shall I, ever again, see with you
The velvet eyes of the Edelweiss
Huddled on hills close to the lake
Where we met with a happy few?
Your furtive glances, cut to size,
For all I knew were not a fake
But to me, drops of euphoria dew . . .
Shall I ever relive such hours with you:
Like flowers plucked at break of youth,
So sweet, halcyon days of truth!
Shall I ever again be with you?

*F Van Haelewyck*

## FALLEN ANGEL

'I shall never forget the weekend Laura died. A silver sun burned
through the sky like a huge magnifying glass. It was the hottest
Sunday of my recollection. I felt as if I were the only human being
left in New York. For Laura's horrible death I was alone.
I Waldo Linkdecker was the only one who really knew her,
and I had just begin Laura's story when another of those
detectives came to see me. I had him wait . . . '

The old man loves Clifton Webb's voice. Summer 1945 he heard it for
the first time, while her fingers toyed with his watchstrap as they
huddled in the second back row of the Orangefield cinema. Feeling
them now he closes his eyes; as the sound echoes around the walls of
the tiny theatre the calmness of the images dance behind his eyes and he almost
sleeps.

*David Blair*


## LOST LOVE

I close
My eyes
And think
Of *You*
Every day
Even now.
I shall
Always
Love *You!*

*John Clare*

## TOGETHERNESS

In the garden of life
the years pass;
The sun and rain
have raised the
seeds of togetherness;
You smile -
And the wind
whispers love;
You reach out
and touch the
contented years
of your belonging.
The tree of togetherness
has grown many
branches,
Whose buds open
to the blossom
of love's wanting.

*Peter Morriss*

## JUST YOU

You are so strong and handsome
So kind and gentle too
That is the reason I married You.
You're always there when I need you,
No-one else would do,
You are so special
I will always love you!
I'm always spending money it's true
Buying clothes that's new.
I'm only trying to look good
Especially for You!

You are so generous
You are so brave
I will always wear the rings
You gave.
The locket and bracelet too
I'll treasure them forever
Just like you!

*Teresa Barnes*

## SQUANDERING TIME

Memories clear glass mirrors our first day
When arm outstretched you clasped my hand in strength
And I first heard your sweet deep tones to say

Your name, and I repeated it at length.
How was I to know our lives would blend
In days to come our hearts entwine, from whence

Came harmony, and I had found a friend.
Brief precious days, fleeting time
In innocence we thought it had no end.

Enriched was life as joys and sorrows chimed
And I never knew just how much you cared
As we sat happily squandering time.

Memory mirrors sweet the hours we shared
Now, too late, I know just how much you cared.

*Jean Carroll*

## MY LOVE

The world receded when my love came
as a wave recedes and leaves the beach.
There was never anyone but him
and suddenly he was out of reach . . .
my love died and left me.

We wove a pattern in years that went
with a bright silken thread running through.
Children and other blessings God sent,
love intertwining the colours true . . .
but he died.

The love and the perfection with flaws,
anger dissolved and freedom to shout.
In life very little room to pause,
the arrogance of time came about . . .
and he died.

Desolation . . . the warmth of skin not there.
Pain and pain and fear of bed space.
Please God, listen to me . . . hear my prayer . . .
please . . . never again to see his face?
Why has he left me?

Now clarity, truth of death it seems,
a birth . . . a beginning it has to be.
I know now . . . I know what Truth means.
He's there . . . patiently waiting for me . . .
With a Love of a greater and wider dimension.

*Dorothy Dowling*

## CATCH ME

Look at me I love you
Catch me in the dancing lights
Like a leaf in the breeze
I will dance, tantalise and take your love
in joy

Touch me I love you
Play in mischief and laugh
Like a rhythm of light
I seek the music in your love
Long into the seasons

Hold me gently I love you
Like a leaf I am turning with time
In the autumn I must die
So catch me now in the dancing lights
now
For tomorrow will be too late.

*Pauline Gee*


## AGEING

Your fear of becoming old
moves me.
Do not be frightened.
I can take off
the delicate threads
of your birthdays
and make you
as young as ever

*Krystyna Lejk*

## PROMISE

I shall go on loving the memory of you.
Of course, it would be easier to try to forget.

But why should I do that? The memory of this love
Is not the love between the sheets, but more passionate.

It is the love that bursts out and flowers
When the friendly sun reflects its rays on you.

It is the love that lasts and lasts,
The love of beauty excavated by the archaeologist in the
sands of time.

It is the love that the Queens of the East,
The Princesses of the pyramids, inspired in their Pharaohs.

It is the love that survives distance, time and loss,
It can be buried but not forgotten.

To know it was there is enough.
It nourishes, it warms, its stretches out hands

And it laughs, it laughs because those who love
Always have the last laugh. They triumph over custom, space and loss.

Open wide blossom. Let the sun kiss you,
As I kiss you, and enter, over time, and space and mystery.

*Bob Fowler*


## A GENTLE LOVE

Ours is a gentle love
That flows as if a singing stream,
Need never seek a lowland plain
And never falls from hills so green.

Ours is a sweetheart's love,
As if that first day dawns again
And when the golden sun does set,
Our tranquil lives remain.

Ours is a romantic love
That swells to music gay
When mellowed by the years that pass,
'Twill still true joy convey.

Ours is that gentle love,
Avoiding peaks and troughs,
Pursuing just one course that's true,
To fill our lives with happy thoughts.

*Brian Harris*


## TO MY SWEETHEART

Good morning my darling,
this card comes to say,
and to tell you I'm well
and my love to convey
to bring back sweet memories
of things that I miss,
your loving arms darling
your caress and your kiss
and to say that I think
the time now draws near
when all that we planned
Will come true my dear
but near or far distant
I'll always be true
I've only one sweetheart
and darling - it's you!

*Annie Gordon*

## LOVE IS . . .

What is love?
A tender kiss?
A sweet embrace?
A swelling ocean?
A raging fire?
Insubstantial as the wind?
As sand through spread fingers?
A force attracting two together?
An animal instinct?
Love is . . .
Oh so many things
Yet refuses to be
Caught like a butterfly,
Killed, pinned,
And neatly classified in Latin.
Mightier than definitions
Love remains,
Always incomprehensible mystery
To the very men
Who talk so much about it.
Age after age men try to understand
Thinking, writing, singing,
Not realising that the final definition
Is already made;
Love is God
For God is love
And love is spelt
*Sacrifice!*

**Anne Thomas**

# A DAY IN THE LIFE OF THE LOVERS

'Good morning dear dear, did I tell you that I love you'. . . she smiled,
          preparation of the bran cereal absorbed her attention.
Together they washed the dishes. His and Hers only now, the sound of the
          radio wafted through the kitchen. 'Nice old song' she said
Now the news 'Fancy that' she murmured. He snorted his disapproval, and
          at furious pace typed a letter to the Times, feelings vented.

The High Street welcomed them. 'So nice to see you.' The shopping trolley
          was obstinate, she rested awhile and gossiped and waved.
He came to meet her, to help her on her way, they paused, looked in
          shop windows, tut-tutted at so many Estate Agents, Charity Shops.
The library was warm, inviting, pretty assistant. A browse through
          some books, a trifle. Well you know. 'Yes we'll have these.'
Friends meeting friends. 'Oh dear are we blocking your way. Sorry about
          your cold.' They dodged away from the friendly germy sneezes.

Then to Mrs Brown, 'No I won't forget the meeting.' She tried to remember
          When where? No she could not remember, not to worry.
The Brown's granddaughter asked. 'Are you really a granny like mine?'
          If you are do you go to sleep for your armchair afternoon rest?
There was no answer to the young questioner just a pat on the head.
          Was it afternoon already? They must try to hurry, food to be prepared.
She said 'Have you got your keys,' then produced hers.

He said 'You know I like your cooking more and more. That was a lovely
          meal.' His waistline was ample proof of her cooking skills.
Rather later for their usual walk which was slow and chilly. It brought
          colour to their cheeks, and an appetite for a snack supper.
What a blessing television was. Vying to answer the Quiz master's questions.
          They were tired and wearily sipped their Camomile tea.
The joy of a warm bed made reading a pleasure, too tired to read more
          They both said 'Did I tell you that I love you?' then fell asleep.

*Grace Graham*

## LOVE AND MARRIAGE

We've been married forty years today
And has it been roses all the way?
Of course it has I say with tongue in cheek
We only had words one day last week
We've had good times, we've had sad
But love always outweighs the bad
No turtle doves are we these days
But love shines out in different ways
A look, a touch, a secret smile.
Keeps me going all the while.
Now love is comfortable like an old shoe
And I know always I can rely on you
The secret of this wedded bliss
Always say goodnight with a kiss
A little tender loving care
A love that we will always share
With two good sons, along the way
Now four grandchildren make our day
You've been my spring, my summer, my autumn too
And in our winter, I'll be there for you.

*Marjorie Pattinson*


## POEMS FOR THE ONE I LOVE

Protective yet not smothering -
You have a certain charm.
By now your hair - it will be grey -
Your voice - a soothing balm.

And O, how you inspire me
With a keen and learned mind.
How you like to talk with me -
You never are unkind

Your eyes - so warm and loving
With many laughter lines -
And shoulders broad enough to take
Our troubles of the usual kinds.

Together with a faith that's strong
And loving life for its beauty.
You can take a serious role
And always do your duty.

Living quietly as I do -
I still am full of elation -
For the one I love whom I have not met
Is just in my imagination.

*Pat Melbourne*


## LONGING

You're so close in my heart
But we're so far apart
And I miss you
The waiting hurts
But it's worth it when I see you
I can hold you and touch you
And you're there.
And partings are so hard
I don't want you to leave
But I have to let you go
Before I see you again.
But the times in between bring me so much pain
Because I love you.
You're so close in my heart,
But we're so far apart
And I miss you

*Nichola Kinnersley*

## MY CHRISTA  (1952)

To me you're like a brilliant sun, when all is black and cloudy
Your sweet face shows between the clouds, you smile and then say howdy
And like a pretty little flower, when everywhere seems dead,
When the earth is hard, and grey and cold, you bow your lovely head.
You're like a cosy fire on a freezing winter's night
When everywhere's completely dark, you're like a shining light,
You are pretty as blossoms and petals in spring,
Like the singing of the birds
Just as an angel from above
With those sweet and charming words.
You are such a lovely person enchanting and petite
And everything about you is so pleasant and so sweet,
Also, very understanding. Have a reassuring way,
You are my only guidance, throughout this world today.
'Tis you that brings me happiness and courage and good cheer,
That's why I love you like I do and hold you very dear.
You are my all and everything and will be all my life,
These are my dear, my reasons, why you're such a perfect wife.
Yes, and such a little darling, and mine all mine alone,
I sometimes wonder, am I worthy of the precious gift I own.
To me you're very precious dear, more so in times like these
You always do your best for me and always try to please.
And that, my own and dearest Chris, is what I think of you,
Just a little consolation, for all the things you do
That's how I see you darling, and has been from the start
You're the highest of the highest, within my eyes sweetheart.

*Peter Sutton*

## ANGELIC HOST PROTECTING

A beam of light harsh and cold dashed across
       the street below,
With no regard for property up the house wall
       it climbed.
It sat on the window ledge waiting for the
       owner to open the curtains,
So it could seep through the glass and play
       shadows in the room beyond.

In the dimly lit room pictures and furniture
       Were outlined along with other flotsam and jetsam,
Slanting off a far wall the light made a pattern
       of the window frame
betwixt lace and cloth.
Hung where this ray of street light thumped
       the wall was a photograph.

It was a large black and white photo of a man
       in his late thirties,
A man with dark questioning eyes that
       stared at you intensely.
A man with a clean shaven jaw proclaiming
       a scar of character.

The shaft of light soft and warm played
       within the room,
Creating a glow around the picture like
       that of an angelic host.
So that while the sleeper rested, a man made
       heavenly light,
Protected the purposely placed picture of
       her heart.

*Heather List*

115

# ONE LIFE, ONE LOVE, ONE FUTURE

It seems to me as I look back
Upon the life I've led so far
That whilst some people something lack
I've lived on love since years before.
The war's cruelty had cast me down
And life for me was one long pain
Yet she had listened without frown
Then brought me back to life again.
My world, misguided, short on love
Had searched and searched for such as she
At times I prayed to God above
As our ship sped across the crashing sea.
A vacuum had descended soon
And stayed until I saw her smile
Her love, her faith, made me reborn
Memories remain, my heart beguile,
Since when we met, my turning point
Life, once dead, began to glow
We were as one, our bodies joint
Oh yes, oh yes, I loved her so.
Now as I sit next evening's gloom
Reflecting yet on days now past
Please, please my love, our life's too soon
I beg you fate please, let it last.
For we will wander hand in hand
Until the final sacrifice
We've had it good, let's join the band
Together then let love survive.

*Cyril Saunders*

## TEARS FOR CRYING

Love is for giving and tears for crying
Hands are fold holding, feet are to walk
Pain is for suffering, love is for trying
Help is for lending, speech is for talk

Friends care and help one another
They're always by your side
Even if it's your sister or brother
They wipe away your tears

Our lives are just one long road
Corner, bends, streets and lanes
In all kinds of weather
We all stick together as friends

Friendship is for a long time
Sometimes this is cut short
Deep down in our hearts and minds
This love cannot never be bought.

*Bambi*

## MY VALENTINE

How I love to kiss your face,
Our bodies touching as we embrace.
In your arms I melt like snow;
My thoughts with you, where're I go
A cake that's iced up to perfection
Can't hold a candle to our affection:
Such a love is yours and mine.
I love you - my Valentine!

*L E Tarplee*

## TO IONA WITH LOVE - FROM A SOUTH COAST BALCONY

A mind-mist takes
These regimented roof-tops
And blossomed avenues
Down to the sea's edge . . .
. . . And I am candlelit in the flute song nave
The Abbey lying still
To contemplate the Sound,
While moon-dressed Mull displays to the star-bright sky
But a dark cross stands behind me.
Will it still bless,
Follow yet,
If I make new communion
With your moon-white face?

*David Knox*


## MY LOVE

I laugh when you laugh, I cry when you cry,
If I couldn't be with you I'd just want to die
I hurt when you hurt, I feel all your pain.
You took over my soul when I took on your name
Though we're two separate beings our hearts beat as one
A wonderful union of our very own.
I draw all my strength from the love that you give
You're my inspiration, my reason to live.
I'll always be true in every way
To the vows that we made on our wedding day
Whatever occurs in the future my dear
We'll face it together without any fear
I'll spend a lifetime trying to prove,
The length and the breadth - the extent of my love.

*Edna J King*

# DREAM MAN

At the first glimpse of your face, I fell quite deeply in love,
My beating heart went soaring as on the wings of a dove.
I dreamed both day and night and gazed out into space,
Every time I looked upon your beloved handsome face.

Your deep sensuous voice sent shivers down my spine,
Your dark velvet eyes had a twinkle and a shine.
I was tempted to run my fingers through your wavy hair,
Just to let you know that I really truly cared.

But alas, you were so famous and I just a blob of a face
In the crowd that followed you everywhere from place to place.
You smiled and waved your manicured hand as if to the manor born,
To all the people in the stands when you came back home.

I filled so many scrap books with pictures just of you,
Year by year I loved you, I was faithful and so true,
I was jealous of the woman that you took for a wife,
So happy when you got divorced, again for single life.

Growing ever handsome as the years passed by,
My heart still fluttered at the twinkle in your eye.
Now the wrinkles started to show upon your changing face,
Dark hair slightly silver yet adding to your grace.

Suddenly the news flashed that we had to part,
I was left alone and crying with my broken heart.
To me you were the King and I your loving Queen,
Beloved Mr Gable the man of all my dreams.

*Eve Clucas*

## FROM ONE FREE SPIRIT TO ANOTHER

I wish I was a flock of gulls shining in the sun,
My love,
Then I could fly to where you are,
If only I could ride their wings to what was once begun,
To what I know is often near, yet far.

To mountain tops, past silver seas,
Through waxing moons to sunset's blaze,
My love,
Your voice will whisper on the breeze,
A memory of different days.

Where birds flit over lawns of grass,
Throwing dark shadows of their wings,
Like memories that rise and pass,
My love,
Of strangely unconnected things.

Call me if you have need or thought,
But not from duty or from my request,
Only if need for me is truly sought,
My love,
Only if love though sorely tried, has passed the test.

I wish I was a beam of golden light,
Something that shines at times for only you,
My love,
A glimmer in your darkest, lonely night,
A spark remaining of what once we knew.

Or, if you tire of things that brightly shine,
I'll be a dark, grey cloud above your head,
My love,
A velvet curtain, drawn dark across the time,
Filling the empty spaces round your bed.

*Kathleen Scatchard*

## SENSES AND FEELINGS

Feelings, tender feelings, emanating beauty that flow so true,
Filling up my senses, with thoughts and actions, sent from you,
Much giving instead of taking, is natural for you all day long,
It makes my heart beat faster, and fills my voice with song.

Strolling and rambling with you, adds further beauty to a sandy shore,
Bringing a tranquillity and peace untold, of hopes and joy in store,
My good fortune was that time I first met you, it seems just a moment ago,
My confidence was re-created, from life's sometimes unearned cruel blow.

Like a perpetual motion of ocean waves, your love ebbs home to me,
On tides of gentle tenderness, born on an endless rolling sea,
Like soft breezes fluttering new-born grass, along a sandy coastal shore,
Where all loneliness departs from within me, who could ask for anything more.

Tides of endless time may take me, beyond places I never knew,
But through all those mists of eternity, I will always yearn for you
This earthly journey is but one lifetime, as I travel on once more,
Your love becomes an eternal key, unlocking each and every door.

I have seen many sights, some made me feel happy, others sad,
But through all those encounters I have made, you are the best I ever had,
Your unselfishness has been a wonder, it has been there for all to see,
A loving part of your natural being, that set my spirit free.

You and I may have lived before, we may through time live again,
We may experience many more emotions, of love, hurt and pain,
Wherever I chance to wander, maybe a pause in time, then reappear,
I know you will always be with me, moving somewhere close or near.

Your love always makes my world turn round, with feelings strong and true,
Always appearing as a world within a world, stimulating deep feelings from
you,
Perpetually filling my senses with tranquil emotions, every passing day,
Forever remaining deep inside my very being, as I quietly pass along my way.

*Jim Wilson*

## MEMORIES

I remember when we first met,
You smiled and said 'Hello'
My heart replied my lips denied,
The thoughts going through my head.

I remember as months went by,
The love that grew inside,
I tried to hide my heart from you,
And loved you better than you knew.

I remember our lives together,
At times the road was rocky,
But as I walked those roads with you,
I loved you better than you knew.

I remember the day you left,
The winter of the year,
You did not see my saddened face,
Nor hear my loud heart beats,
And as you walked 'til out of view,
I loved you better than you knew.

I remember my dreams of you,
I watched you as a star,
But as a star you're out of reach,
So in my dreams I say to you,
I loved you better than you knew.

*Ann Smith*

## FATHER

I remember those days when I was young
The things we did, having lots of fun
I remember that day you ran a mile
When my nappy was changed you didn't smile.
I can never forget when I sat on your knee.
You taught me to clap, you looked so happy.
I remember the day you took my hand.
You made me walk you made me stand.
I can never forget the cinema trips
Sweets under the pillow and sherbet pips.
I remember the time sweet whispers were said.
If I held on to you, then I was scared I guess.
I remember those days I sat on your shoulder,
I wish I was young don't want to grow older.
You took me to school, to the parks and shops,
My love for you will never stop.
If you look very carefully, you'll see yourself in me
A joint personality, without it I'm incomplete
How can I repay you, for what you've done for me?
You're not only my Father but as a friend should be
So listen up my Dad, to what I have to say
I thank God each morning for bringing you my way.

*Ashie Rana*

## FIRST LOVE

The ghost of your kiss
Upon my cheek
Wakes me as the sun caresses
My exposed skin.
I reach out
To find the imprint of your body.
Your heat reaches my fingers
From crumpled sheets.
As I turn and smell
The scent of you,
Your touch lingers on.
The silence bears down upon me.
I long for your heartbeat
Against mine.
The weight of you,
The feel of your body,
The pleasures of your flesh.
I call to you in the
First light of morning,
Fearing you have deserted me,
Hating you, loving you, needing you.
Your answer is silence and
I ache inside at my loss.
But as I seek to understand your absence
Your voice melts me as
You smile from the open doorway
And all is forgiven.

*Rachel M Jones*

## THE LIGHT

When visiting in that dream-like place
That exists within my own mind's eye
I came upon one barren plain
And one boundless storm stressed sky,
All around was drear and dark
A dense mist hugged the weathered ground
And in my heart there grew a fear
That to stay meant not to be found,
In the distance hung a shimmering light
That weakly shone yet strongly too,
It called to me and beckoned me
As if my pain it knew.

My legs were weighted by invisible chains
I struggled forward ever on
Straining towards the distant light
That pure and solid shone,
It seemed I walked for many miles
Sometimes the light would dance away
But if I fought unto the last
I knew the light would stay,
All at once the light was mine
At peace I stood completely still,
And let the warmth enter my soul
To chase away the chill.

I looked back on the storm filled sky
That rained tears on the plain named misery
And knew the light to be a smile
That my sweet love had sent to me.

*Bronwyn Lewis*

## SECOND CHANCE

How can I tell you how it feels?
To know how gently someone touches
With caring hands and gentle fingers
That make me tingle with desire!
To feel and kiss a gentle man
Who means so well and knows so little
Love.
The danger is to love too much,
To let go feelings of such fire!
The power to stop is almost none
When two people's hearts need so much fun!
No one to care for, no one to care . . .
Is something now, we can't compare
With how it was before . . .
Before the strong attraction was confirmed
And loving thoughts began to burn!
To strongly hold and love so much.
To feel the tingle from a tender touch!
The hormones free are racing round
Raising our *feet* off the ground!
The after-glow is with me still.
With obvious joy my eyes soon fill
With gleaming light of loving thoughts
That knowing you, to me has brought!

*Muriel Hughes*

126

## A LOVER'S POEM

Love me my darling,
As I love you
Love me for what I am
And not for what I do.

I will never leave you darling,
Because it just isn't in me,
I will stay with you forever,
Just you wait and see.

Our love is too strong,
For us to ever part
I've loved you since we met,
From the very start.

So stay here by my side,
Each and every day
I'll show you the way to happiness,
I will show you the way.

Just hold me my sweetheart
Hold me very tight,
I will stay with you forever
Every day, and every night.

*Stephanie Harvey*

## MY DARLING

Did I ever tell you, how special that you are?
How I longed to hold you, while gazing from afar.
Your body used to haunt me, every day and night.
Just to pass near by you, set my passion all alight.

Remember how fate played its very tricky part,
Giving us the chance to let our friendship start.
How we used to stroll on those blissful summer nights.
Letting love grow stronger as we sampled its delights.

Finally telling your parents of our strong love's bond
Planning for our wedding, when you dad gave me your hand.
Then starting life together in that first home that we shared.
Planning for a family, one girl and boy is all we dared.

Laughing how nature tricked us, by supplying twins.
Making it a struggle, to buy two of all the things.
Watching as they grew, from babies to their teens,
Then letting them both go to start their life of dreams.

So now we are alone again, just like we started out
Now I want to tell you, Oh! I really want to shout!
And tell the world I love you, My darling how I care.
So thank you for your love dear, and letting me your life share.

*George Bailey*

**TO BE IN LOVE**

To be in love
is a new window
on an old world
where every dawn
is a vision of gold,
that fills each day
with wonder and light
makes magic of darkness
and glows through the night.

Each lover's heart
like an ancient temple
stands in time
filled with beauty and fire
where archways lead
to the secret centre.
There burns the flame
that is never extinguished
the lantern that glows
from the high temple ceiling,
swaying aloft with each turn of earth
where two lovers consummate
fire in their knowing
in holding and joining
in giving and loving.

*Margaret Gibian*

## MILES

I love your gentle smile
the warmth of your embrace
I love your starlit eyes
and that look upon your face

I love the way you laugh
I love the way you talk
I love the way you frown
and I love the way you walk

I love your slender body
your muscles well defined
love your many expressions
love your heart, soul and mind

I love that spell you put on me
As you sweetly kiss my lips
love that wonderful sensation
flowing from your fingertips

I love the way you joke about
and how we pretend to fight
love the way you keep me warm
on the darkest, coldest nights

I love everything about you
I know we'll never part
you have a very special place
deep within my heart.

*Rachel Kearton*

## THE STORY OF MY WIFE

You came my way, that day in June,
When all the world, was so in tune
I knew so little of you then
Or, what was hidden from my ken.
Yet e'er that day, had turned to night.
My lonely fears, had taken flight.
I'd found the girl to win my heart
To share my world, till death do part.

You were warm and kind, faithful too.
You made my wildest dreams come true.
Close by my side, if things went wrong
Your hand in mine made me feel strong.
And as we walked along life's way,
You added treasures to each new day
How on that day your love I'd find,
Good fortune, that to me was kind.

And sharing in our homely bliss,
Was our very own, special Miss.
Her love for us, brought us joy
And angel ways, were her ploy.
So happy were those days we shared,
Because unashamedly we cared.
As if all this was meant to be,
The day you gave your love to me.

The years rolled on as was their due,
Our love remained, as ever true.
But ageing, must bring forth its fears
And ill health came in later years.
Still by your side, we bravely stood.
Repaying you, as best we could.
Yet God above, knew what was best
And granted you, Eternal Rest.

*George Allen*

## LOVE AT A DISTANCE

Snowflakes, pure white snowflakes,
how I wish I were favoured as they
gently, lightly caressing your cheek
lingering
soft as a kiss upon your lips
spreading a carpet for your feet
you stand
face uplifted to receive their touch
whilst I, with longing
stand at a distance, afraid and shy.

Breezes, cool fresh breezes
how I wish I were forward as they
teasing, impishly tousling your hair
whispering
songs of springtime in your ears
painting roses in your cheeks
you pause
breathless, awaiting their embrace
whilst I, with yearning
stand at a distance and faintly sigh.

### *Elizabeth Peacock*

## LOVE

A story of love, perhaps the best there is
words from the heart, each gentle kiss,
walking beneath the stars above,
two people, sharing a deep tender love.

### *Tom Ginn*

# GRANDCHILDREN

When I was a callow youth, I learned never to try
To solve life's sweet mystery, or ask the great God, why?

When young there was one joy, to which I did aspire,
A trip to the Music Hall, a tuppenny seat at the Empire.
Wonderful artists I saw, but I never knew their name,
For the programme sellers never to the gallery came.

One beautiful lady singer, with a sweet and haunting tone,
I remember singing a sad ballad, aptly entitled 'Alone'
   'Alone on a night, that was meant for love, there
    must be someone waiting who feels the way I do'
By bitter experience, I found these words were seldom true
'Oft I've lingered lonely, when the moon was crystal clear.
Awaiting for that someone waiting, who never did appear.

Then a red nosed comic, or perhaps his nose was blue,
Said he had solved the mystery and swore it was true
For he sang:
   'Oh! Sweet mystery of life at last I've found you
   Oh! At last I've found the secret of it all'
He then produced a wacking long string of - Sausages,
So I knew . . . He didn't know at all.

Then a wonderful thing happened, in my advancing years
Four lovely Grandchildren, just suddenly appears.
They took me by their little hands and led me to their wonderland
I thank whatever Gods may be, but will never understand.
Like the callow youth of yester-year, I will not even try
To solve life's sweet mystery, or ask the great God, Why?

*Philip Williams*

## LOVE TO YOU DEAR

Life is a necklace of memories
So when things aren't as they seem.
Finger a bead and close my eyes.
Then allow myself to dream.

At first I never cared for you
You were always one to rove.
But when you returned, suddenly I knew
We were truly and deeply in love.

I can still see your face as I walked up the aisle
In the same dress worn by my mother.
Like you, I knew our guests were there.
But we only had eyes for each other.

Happily we were blessed with three children.
Can't believe how the time has flown.
They all married too and we were grandparents
Like us, for them joy was known.

My dear, you're no longer with me
I smile at your empty chair
We shared a wonderfully total thing
It's easy to pretend you're sat there.

I feel you are with me always my dear
You made our life such a thrill
And so until we meet again
I love you and always will.

*Violette Edwards*

## MY LOVE

My love,
He is a wonder
And I'll never let him go.

My love,
He's so special
And I want to let him know.

My love,
Listens carefully
To every word I say

My love,
I love so much,
In every possible way

My love,
Comforts me when I'm sad
And shares my happiness with me.

My love,
Is always on my mind,
In whatever I do or see.

My love
Makes me feel special
By showing me his love is true

My love,
Neil,
I want you to know
That I love you too!

*Louise Naylor*

## WITH MY LOVE

I've loved you now for
     so many years
Sharing love, happiness
     and tears
My lover, friend and
     husband too
I couldn't have made
     it through life without you

Always there when I
     needed you most
Ready to give and not
     count the cost
Our love has grown
     stronger as the years
Have rolled by
     Years shared together
Just you and I

God gave us this gift
     this gift of love
His special gift from
     heaven above
And we have shared
     this love together
Side by side whatever
     the weather.

Because of our love
     so special to you and me
We produced a family
     of three
And they in return
     have done their share
Giving us love to show
     how they care.

So thank you for all the
      love given to me in life.
From the one who is proud
      to be your wife.

*Marjorie Ridley*


## A FOOL'S GAME

Don't think because I pack your bags
I don't want you to stay
Or that taking down your photo
Drives our memories away,
Don't think because we argue
That I love you any less,
It's just that I get angry
If the house is in a mess,
And if after a beer you're told
Your dinner's in the cat,
It's just because I've missed you
So take no notice of that,
Thinking of the hours spent
We've shouted bullied cursed,
Ignoring all the good times
By just dwelling on the worst,
So don't be hurt by silly games
We foolish lovers play,
Because my darling, I love you
Much more than words can say.

*Sarah Maycock*

## LOVE CAN ONLY GAIN

Every girl has a place
In her heart there's a space
That lovely smile that lovely face
She walks with such heavenly grace.

The gloomy night of sorrow
Raving night that knows tomorrow
Her friendship makes me blest
My urge is my one request.

I believe in the Kingdom come
Where two loves bleed into one
We broke the bonds, loosened the chain
Now our sweet love can only gain.

*Philip Anthony Corrigan*


## TO MY LOVE

Our love is a shared expectation
For a future together planned
A rose given and accepted
A walk on the beach hand in hand

Love is hopes and plans and dreams
All rolled up in a shiny ball
To catch and hold till the end of time
Together in spite of it all

Love is floating high on a cloud
In skies that are always blue
But when the dark storm clouds gather
Sun will shine through while I still have you.

*Peggy Hunter*

# A WHIRLWIND COURTSHIP

Do you remember the weekend we met?
You came to see the Falls and found me.
Me, wearing ragged jeans and vest.
You, riding the biggest bike I'd ever see.

Do you remember that first meal we ate?
You strung beans while I cooked mince.
They must have been aphrodisiac
for we've been deep in love ever since.

That was Friday, I'd bought a new car
Vowing love was for others not me.
Well, vowing didn't get me very far!
Monday you proposed under a green leafed tree.

I couldn't believe my ears, this was mad.
For it was only two days since we'd met.
Now it's twenty-five years since we married
and we're not bored with each other yet.

Do you remember those sparkling drops,
flung in the air by the thundering Falls,
as we sat side by side in stark wonderment.
Blown apart by the speed of it all.

As a gift you bought me a drum not a ring
from the traders' stalls near to the Falls.
The taut cowhide skin makes music still
like my heart at the sound of your call.

### *Janis Priestley*

**IN THE AFTER YEARS**
*(Dedicated to A.D)*

If I could write a love song
I would dedicate to you
The words my heart would whisper
So tender and so true.
I would tell the deepest ocean
And every greenwood tree
The extent of my devotion
For all eternity.

If I could write a love song
To express my dearest dream
I would set the words to music
With melody supreme.
Loves wild theme would blossom
And to our hearts respond
In the after years together
Forever and beyond.

*Mary Ferguson*




**OTHERWISE ENGAGED**

Dear Joe,
To draw, and paint a masterpiece,
        That's what I want to do,
And tend my little garden
        On days when skies are blue
To practice on my violin
        Perfect notes, so pure and true
And, on dad's old piano,
        Compose a tune or two.

140

Yet, I'm making crochet lace now,
  And fine embroidery do,
Attending cookery classes -
  So I'll be useful too,
I'd hoped to become quite famous,
  To serve my genius true!
If only I could clear my mind
  Of loving thoughts of you!

**Betty Adams-Mailey**


## A ROSE WROUGHT IN BLUE FIRE

Pale beauty through a mystic glass
And elfin firelight - dreams that pass
Like shadows of the questing self
The half seen vision of an elf;
So gentleness, that of a fawn
Is unknown light beyond the dawn,
And hues that only Angels scan -
Soft imprints on perceptive man,
A laser-light bestowed by Gods
Who touch the soul with lightning rods!
The barest trace - a petalled line,
Might pass from thought, or seem divine
Before an unseen spark grows cold
A Seraph's creed turns it to gold.
And might a rose wrought in blue fire
Be Shelley's vision of desire?
Or in a star-shower of the heart
Might Keat's worth be the noblest art?

**Christopher Rothery**

## MY LOVE - MY LIFE

Dedicated to the man in my life - simply to express
How much I love you so, you are my happiness
To me you are my love, my life, my everything
Being with you makes my heart dance and sing.

You bring sunshine to my days, passion in the night
Your kisses thrill me so, fill me with delight
You walked into my life one bright day in May
You charmed me so; you stole my heart away

Lady luck smiled on us, giving us a chance
We fell head long, 'twas love at first glance
Our eyes met: instantly we both felt the inclination
Now my darling you are my one true inspiration.

Tenderly you hold me in your arms so strong
Convincing me forever that, that's where I belong
All alone with you, down comes my walls of defence
Under your captive spell my submission you sense

Together we are lifted to the heights of sensation
My head is spinning round in wild intoxication
With you I'm all woman, you are all man
I'll do for you anything that I possibly can

Giving you all that your heart could ever desire
Hoping that somehow, together our dreams will aspire
That one day you'll ask me to be your loving wife
In happiness together we'll walk the path of life.

Over the threshold with you, whisked off my feet
Soon we'll start a family to make our life complete
A baby boy for you a baby girl for me
And we'll all live together in perfect harmony.

*Carol Anne Burnup*

## FOR HARRY, OR I WROTE A LETTER TO MY LOVE

Who am I that I should want to hold you,
Closer than the everlasting arms.
When my morning-waking eyes no longer see
Your dear face,
Perhaps you see mine.

Only in memory may I hear your voice,
Yet your love lives for me in little loves,
Wild bird song, roses scent,
The quiet thoughts of evening,
A well-loved room, where we have sat together,
holding hands, the warmth of lingering love
that never lets that room grow cold.
Dear heart, we are together still and one day shall be closer
than this world can ever know.
Dear heart, for you and me there is no death
God would not part whom He hath joined together.

*Hilary Mason*


## IF

If I touch your fingers
Where my mind touched long ago
I will see within your shining eyes
Whether to stay or go.

If I kiss your soft, sweet lips
Then I will surely know
How your thoughts have strayed there
Helping mine to grow.

If I hold you in my arms
With the glow of love's pure light
I will keep you there my darling
For this and every night.

*David Tas*

## REFRAIN

Overtures lilt through the letter box
Silver tongued melodies; bound in black.
Nostalgic notes that air memories
Of satin sheets . . . and mourning.

The syllables strike chords of past harmonies
When bodies moved in tune.
A siren's song of silver words
On a tide of emotion lures

Enveloping in a symphony of sensation.
Ends crashing in a crescendo of pain
As dreams founder on the rocks of reality
Again . . . and again.

*Lee Thomas*

## FRIEND

Friend,
Friend if we are in the rain and get wet
There is no lasting pain:
The wet weather does not hurt permanently
Even if we catch a cold or flu.

Friend if we are in the sun
And we do not feel the need
To draw others into the radiance
To share the warmth, to rejoice together
To dance, there is deep pain,
As women and men are meant
        For unity and communion.

If I do not communicate with you
I will die of silence.

*Angela Matheson*

144

## LOVE

Love, is it something that blinds you?
    With its amazing light.
    Or is it like a flame?
    Which flickers, yet burns so bright.

Does it make us silly -
    Enthusiastic or dumb?
    Making us change everything,
    For that loving one.

Does it hit you suddenly?
    Or grow with hope and care?
    Does it happen to everyone?
    With whose life you share.

Why is it we suffer?
    Just so we can see,
    That person get through their life
    So very easily.

And even when we're left alone,
    Broken by the love that's gone.
    Why is it we'll go through all of it,
    Just to find someone?

*Sarah Lucy Dunkley*

## DREAMING OF LOVE

When I was young, I dreamt of love.
Of words that rang like the cries of seagulls,
Carried on the breeze.
Or the hush of the wind up high
Twisting and rustling the leaves.

When I was young, I dreamt of love,
Of kisses that pull, wanting to devour,
Like the lapping waves on the sand.
Of a butterfly bending the stalk of a flower,
As gentle as the stroke of his hand.

When I was young, I dreamt of love.
Of a heat that thunders and sighs
As I lie cool and limp in the marble room.
My eyes reflected in his eyes,
As water mirrors the passive moon.

When I was young, I dreamt of love
And thought I was wishing too much.
But you have stood higher
Than I could ever dream.

*Lorraine Phillips*

## LOVE

What is love? What does it mean.
How do you explain it - can it be seen?
When do you know you've got it,
How does one keep it alive?
All of us say 'Yes I love you,'
But does it exist and really survive.

You can't touch it, or smell it
Feel its size, here it call.
We are told love one another - love thy neighbour
Love us all . . .
We read about it, see it at the pictures
Some folk boast of loves sweet dream,
But do they really understand its meaning . . .
Can they explain what true love means?

I call it more a feeling
Warm, safe, happy, excitement
To name a few.
This I have felt so strongly,
Since first I was introduced to you.
So that's *My Love*, how I explain it
The things I feel, how best I see
This wondrous, wondrous feeling
Of all the love I have for thee.

*Pam Stennett*

## THE CANDLE

I knew there was something wrong my dear
I felt it in my heart.
So much for everyone else's words
They said we'd never part.

They saw the light shine brightly,
The eternal light of life.
The light that would bring happiness,
To make us man and wife.

But as they were not watching
The candle light grew dim.
And before they knew what was happening
'She was crying over him'.

As my candle flickered
The heart broke from the wax
My candle fell so quietly,
For fear light won't be coming back.

The Lord he acts in mysterious ways
He said 'Let there be light.'
The candle shone again that day
But will it ever shine as bright?

It was an optical illusion.
It wasn't candle light that glowed.
A shadow fell across my heart
And again my tears flowed

*Angela Hughes*

## LATE LAST NIGHT

Before returning home
late last night,
You took me to a castle on a hilltop
and opened the skylight
and the stars fell in;
You are
not of this world.

In your room,
upon opening the cupboards
I found them full of butterflies
and a rainbow ended on your pillow.

And this morning,
seeing you, heart still,
body blushing with light,
it seems suddenly that my head is full of dragons
and my chest with cherry blossom.

*Katherine Baldwin*


## A KISS!

A kiss to say good morning
A kiss that seems so right
A kiss to say I thank you
A kiss to say goodnight.

A kiss that notes our friendship
A kiss once in a while
A kiss that shows we're happy
A kiss and then a smile.

A kiss that tells no lies
A kiss to show it's true
A kiss to say three words
A kiss to say I love you!

*Graham Mitchell*

## POEM FOR JON

I loved you when you were 19
henna red hair
tight trousers
smooth chest
ambitious
tender
puppy

I love you now age 34
husband
proud father
of our miracle cherub son
ambitious
tender
man

*Penny Stempel*

## LOVE FOREVER

I love you
I really do
Perhaps we'll see another year through.
When we're settled, what do you think,
A Blessing in Church, will make us ring true.

Over the hills and over the dales,
My love for you will never die,
It will strengthen from day to day,
So what do you say,
Can we have our day?

*Mary Jo West*

## MY HUSBAND AND I

My husband and I we were married 41 years ago
We had a quiet white wedding, not a big show,
Our friends were invited and family too,
We thought everything would be perfect as you usually do.

After our honeymoon in Jersey we returned to live in a flat,
We were both working hard, trying to save for this and that,
We came down to earth and realised it wasn't much fun,
When we were both working shifts, there was a lot to be done.

We both dreamed of a house a garden and children too,
But things didn't work out as we wanted it to do,
There was many trials and problems galore,
But somehow we stayed together through it all.

We adopted four children, 2 boys and 2 girls from a home,
As we found we couldn't produce and have our own,
We managed to survive all pressures, trials as before,
The little ones given to us was our anchor, giving us love,
                          who could ask for more.
So life carried on year after year,
We had obtained our ready made family, they provided laughter and tears,
Through schooldays and holidays we were united together as one,
There is nothing like family life, children can be much fun.

Now we are alone once more, our children are all gone,
Left home to make their own lives, forging ties as we have done,
We now have grandchildren who love us we are known as Grandad and Nan,
I guess life is so good if we follow God's plan.

The secret to life lies in the ability to freely love,
It does not come easy, but we learned to trust and listen to our Father above,
Good marriages are made in heaven, we have to learn to give and take,
No one is perfect and if we try, think carefully, we will find our true mate.

*J M Collinson*

## A PERFECT STRANGER

You often share my dinner
although you never eat.
When you come into my home
we never really meet.

You're tall and very handsome
stylish and 'Tres Chic'.
With a charm that's easy going
you make my knees go weak.

A knight in shining armour
To the rescue you ride.
Fighting crime and injustice
with a beauty at your side.

When it comes to romance
you're really quite sublime.
But that's not so surprising
since you do it all the time.

Unlike others of your sex
you're gentle and polite.
There's never any danger
that you would start a fight.

You would never stand me up
or leave me feeling down.
You're not the kind of person
who ever wears a frown.

You're a perfect stranger
the ideal man for me.
To see you all I have to do
is turn on my TV.

*Joanne Smith*

152

## ANNIVERSARY ROSE

A single rose, I cut this day
The petals soft, as velvet lay
Its scent was strong, sweet, divine
As I placed it by a glass of wine.

I raised my glass, in silent toast
To an absent friend, I love the most
Absent long, so sorely missed
Unable to be, at our table tryst.

Into my wine, there falls a tear
I speak the words, she loved to hear
'I love you,' I whisper, softly say
And backhanded, wipe the tears away.

I placed the rose, in water clear
By her photograph, I put it near
A sad smile to her eyes, I'm sure appears
I smile back, through my tears.

*Bill Vass*

## LOVE LINES

They were tied in a bundle with ribbon of blue
At the end of each letter the words I love you
They are not just words in a letter apart
They are feelings that come straight from the heart
So tie up the ribbon and put them away
Love lines not forgotten but remembered each day

*Thelma Hynes*

## I LOVE YOU ALAN PRATT

It was inevitable
That I loved you
Even before we met.

You call it chance:
I'll call it destiny.

We were exactly where
We had to be:
      In space
      In time
      In experience,
For us to be the people
We are today:
For our relationship to work.

Will you share,
      Be part of,
      My reality?
I Love you Alan Pratt!

*Carole House*




## MY LOVE IS TRUE

To only you, my love I give,
you're the one I want to be with,
my tender kisses are only for you,
as you know darling, my love is true.

You are the love in my heart,
I can't bear it when we're apart,
I love the things you say and do,
as you know darling, my love is true.

I'm torn apart when you have to leave,
when I say I love you, please believe,
my heart is yours, my body too,
as you know darling, my love is true.

Sending my love on this Valentine's day,
as this poem tells you in every way,
I want to spend my life with you,
as you know darling, my love is true.

*Anna Green*


## EVERMORE

The wind blows gently, through the trees
Whispering softly, amongst the leaves,
As I walk on afraid no more
On towards the open door.

I enter slowly, silently perhaps
And glance around for any trace,
That you have been here, once before,
Through the ever open, welcoming door

I look around and there I see
Head bowed, down upon knee,
My favourite love, the one I adore,
Is here for me, evermore.

*Eilidh Macpherson*

## HIS DAY WITHOUT ME

We are almost always together
But today he went off on his own,
He went to Bury with some of his pals,
And I was left all alone.
I thought about him all day long
Not one minute was he out of my mind,
I pictured him there, in Bury,
I was sad that he'd left me behind.
I felt as though I'd lost my leg
Or that a chunk of me had gone,
I longed for him to come home again,
And I prayed that he wouldn't be long.
He said he'd be home around seven,
I hoped he wouldn't be late,
I tried to watch telly, but couldn't
So I sat by the window to wait.
Suddenly there he was at the gate
And I felt a sense of relief,
How very much I'd missed him today
Was quite beyond belief.
He said he'd had a lovely day
And I was glad that he had,
Next time I'll try to go with him
And then we'll both be glad.

*Rose Coote*

## WEDDING ANNIVERSARY

I dreamed a dream one day
A Prince took me away -
A man so good and kind
He stole this heart of mine!

I dreamed a dream one night
I did on wings take flight
From bombs and noise and war
All this for me was o'er.

My dreams - they both came true -
That night when I met you!
A Prince you've ceased to be
You're now a King to me!

The years have made you so
As onward we both go -
Our life has brought much pain
Yet o'er it all - *You Reign!*

*Jeanne Boffey*


## SEEKER

I long to walk the beach again
To view the restless sea,
To breathe the salty air and then
Watch sea birds soaring free.

The wind shall blow away my fears
And set the waves in motion,
But sea shells murmur in my ears,
'You'll never cross the ocean!'

Alas 'tis true, I'll stay ashore,
My love, I fear, is gone
To lie in sleep forever more,
Though he and I were one.

157

Roll on you vasty ocean deep
Caress the golden sand,
I know my love can wake from sleep
When God will take his hand.

And so I'll walk the beach again
To view the restless sea,
To breathe the salty air, and then
My love will come to me.

*E Balmain*


## OPIUM

Sweet memories of love's first fleeting touch
when music times the beating of the heart
and aromatic markers show us much
of chemical dependence at its start.

If seeds could boost that bloom of summer love,
which drug would hold that moment in array?
Which opiate could wear the silken gloves
that keep approaching autumn signs at bay?

If we could hold the tenderest of times,
which one of us would not addicted be?
But I can only hold them in my rhymes
and keep a fond nostalgia in my dreams

And though succeeding winters are unkind,
your summer freshness wanders through my mind.

*John Tirebuck*

## A STRAND OF HAIR

As I look upon you,
I see a strand of hair,
Curling down,
Resting lightly,
On your forehead.

I wish that I could raise my hand,
And gently brush aside,
The straying lock,
The silken strand,
That lies there.

But sitting in a crowded room, with friends on either side,
I am powerless,
To make the move,
To make you mine,
Forever.

Then suddenly, you return my gaze with eyes that know,
With a look that shares,
The tender torture
The sweetened sadness,
Of my dilemma

At last I know they way you feel!
A gentle spell descends,
Dancing lightly,
Singing softly,
Without a sound.

Wordlessly you give consent,
I raise a weightless hand,
Without a thought,
Without a care,
I brush aside the strand.

*P M Holloway*

## MY LOVELY BLUEBELL GIRL

There's a lovely, lonely, flower called the *'Bluebell'*
'Tis as dear to my heart as anything,
Because it never, never, fails just to remind me,
Of the girl who won my heart, 'twas in the spring.

To see that lovely *'Bluebell'* in the shadows,
As it nestles there, beneath those mighty lofty trees,
Or to see it there, in sunshine on the hilltop,
As it visited, by hordes of bumble bees.

To watch it there among the thorns and thickets,
As it sways there, in the gentle summer breeze,
Or to see it, in a storm of hail and thunder,
My lovely *'Bluebell'* flower, remains the same to me.

Please look at the *'Bluebell',* next time you see one,
And examine most carefully, every little bell,
You find each one, will make you fully welcome,
To come closer and still closer, its beauty others tell.

Robbie Burns, may write about his *'Highland Mary'*
Sir Harry Lauder, sing of his *'Heather'* in the dell,
But I'll say without fear of contradiction,
I'll win the race, hands down, with my *'Bluebell'*.

She has passed through storms, and disappointments,
Many heartbreaks, she has borne there all alone,
Yet she's still the same, the beautiful little *'Bluebell'*
That I met, in my home town, many years ago.

God knows, for how many years, she's been tormented,
Still my love for her, has never, never changed,
I only wish, I could have helped to share those burdens,
My lovely *'Bluebell',* those dreams to rearrange.

Ere my pen is set down could be forever,
Behind each tear there is a lovely little smile,
Back of each cloud there is a silver lining
It helps me over all those weary miles.

I will finish here my *'Bluebell'* with one thought,
That for you and I our love has brought,
A tenderness, a beautiful inward feeling,
That love will still, go on living.

*David Hancock*


## WHEN I THINK OF YOU

What I feel now
when I think of you
is not the lightning flash
or urgent love
but the radiance deep
of the summer sun
lasting long
and warming through and through.

The goddess of golden youth
that you were
has become as well as lover
fellow striver, friend
and children's mother.
All the things we have been
are bound together
in what we are.
As our seasons grow
All the love that we knew
is more than ever
real and alive
in the love we know.

*David Poole*

## TO MY DEAREST

When I saw you in the morning
Snoring slightly by my side
Not so perfect, my Adonis,
Yet for me and mine by right.

How I snuggled close for comfort
As your breath tickled my ear.
Your strong arms surrounded me,
Banishing forever fears.

How it amused me to watch you
As you rubbed sleep from your eyes
And still half asleep you'd kiss me
As you took me towards the skies.

Then came breakfast as I loved it
While you showered I made tea.
And I sang to show the world
That you belonged to me.

But where are you now my dearest?
How I miss those little snores.
What has happened my Adonis,
That you left and I can feel your arms no more.

*Mariella Cassar*

## CAROL

My girlfriend's name is Carol
I've known her many years
And in that time we've shared a lot
Of laughter, joys and tears
She lives up in Fintry
I live in the town
But I see her quite a lot
She always comes down

She sits like a lady
While I make our tea
But she washes all the pots
And dishes up for me

We talk about our children
And how they're getting on
It seems they're hardly with you
Then they're up and gone

Now we are proud grandparents
And we spoil them all
And at the Christmas holidays
They really had a ball

And to see them happy
Made us happy too
I love them all so very much
And Carol, I love you!

*David Wilson*

## INNER THOUGHTS

I used to laugh and feel alive
But now I just feel dead inside
When I'm with you I can't let myself go
You say you love me but that can't be so.

I used to have so many dreams
But you said I was foolish or so it seems
When I'm with you I do nothing right
Now my face is darkened where once it was bright.

I used to be so young at heart
But you said I acted like a silly young tart
When I'm with you I feel so old
My love for you has now grown cold.

I used to hope one day you would change
But alas, it was my life you rearranged
When I'm with you I'm crying inside
Now in my middle years I have to decide.

Should I break with you and let it all out
Be foolish and silly, scream and shout
Find happiness, before it's too late
Will I have the courage, what will be my fate?

*Ann Richardson*

## LOVES BOND ETERNAL

Make it where the whispering seas
Kiss the shores perpetual
Where the wavelets sweet caress
Brings us warmth, and secret dreams,
And tender, loving kindness.

Make it where the gentle wind
Sings of forever and for love.
Under triumphant sunset skies -
Our hands, our lips, our voices,
And the love that fills our eyes.

Make it where infinity
Leaves us walking, hand in hand
For ever after, and before -
Our loves bond eternally.
Just this, and nothing more

*Alison Robertson*


## TOGETHER

I dreamed a wondrous dream last night
For oh! I found *you* there,
I held you and hugged you tight
And stroked your red-gold hair
I kissed your lips, kissed your eyes,
I kissed away your tears
I felt your heartbeat, heard your sighs,
And gently calmed your fears.
We were together, you and I,
As we had always been
Bound by a love that cannot die
Though death may intervene.

*John Millar*

## LOVE

Love -
You are my life
I breathe you in
And bathe in your glow

Love -
You are my sun
My moon and my stars
You shine on me

Love -
You are my heart
My mind and my soul
I live just for you

Love -
You are  flowing through me
We are flowing together
Into eternity

Love -
Together it's heaven
Hold me -
And I'll take you there . . .

*Sue Lightfoot*


## THE KISS

Linger with a kiss my love,
Let me feel the bliss my love,
I shall leave the earth my love
Thinking I'm in Heaven above
But on earth I will really be
With you, my love, my destiny
          In ecstasy!

*Margaret Carter*

## DEDICATION

Dulcet tones caress my mind
Troubles melt away.
Sweet contentment is, I find,
In the things you say.

Favours sought are not denied.
Nothing bothers you.
Trust and hope your constant guide
In all the things you do.

Love can conquer everything,
Remove an ugly scar.
Introduce a breath of spring;
For that is what you are.

Dedication throughout life,
The trigger and the key.
Devotion from a treasured wife,
Who means so much to me.

*Stan Taylor*


## THE DANCE OF LIFE

Across a room I've seen your face
And in my heart reserved a place
So why not come and daily dine
And be my annual Valentine!

*H Maybee*

# THE SENSUOUS COUPLE

Surreal and radiant in ethereal light
She stands aglow, virginal, in white.
Posing maturely as any woman might
Whose younger years have taken flight.

Composed, she smiles to one who stands
Apart, unsure but proud to unhand
His vision of loveliness as she stands
Twixt modern Ms. and wedding band.

Her confident smile shortens their distance,
Draws them closer, senses a-dance.
Eyes only for each, they're in a trance,
Totally oblivious to their audience.

Grasping hands, flowers between
Their tangible magic can be seen.
'Dear dad, I love and thank you to have been
So loving and caring, our homely scene.'

As my husband gulped, the camera caught
Their visible emotions, high and taut.
Hugs and kisses, handkerchiefs sought -
'Come on dad, let's go in, I think we ought.'

*Jennifer Wright*

## TOM

What did Tom mean to me?
Fun, happiness, tranquillity.
There were no shallow edges,
A deep, still lake,
On which I floated with content.

We shared our lives,
We created our family.
Tom - borne from love
Gave love, received love
And will eternally live
In His father's love.

His family - Precious legacy live on;
Creating fun, happiness, tranquillity
Remembering the deep, still lake,
On which they floated with content.
Learning to love and be loved
For eternity.

*Sheila Eadie*


## THE YOU I LOVE

I can but praise
The you, you are
With me through all my darkest days
You've always been my star
Your tender, loving, caring ways
Helped me come this far.

*Michael Wixon*

## LOVE SO DEEP

Deep in my heart
Love is burning bright
Even though
We are far apart

Miles away
From your warm embrace
No more lips
To kiss my face

No hands to hold
No face to touch
No more loving
Tender touch

Sweet thoughts
Of you
My heart comes alive
Loves burning bright
Deep down inside

A glow and a glimmer
Is all I see
When I think
Of what
You mean to me

*Margaret J Franklin*

## MY WIFE IS MY LIFE

*(A dedication to my dear wife Kathleen, a loving wife for the past thirty three years)*

As I sit down at the end of another year, my thoughts they start to play,
I think of all my wife has done, it's more than words can say,
How lucky I am to be her husband, she sees when I am down,
A soothing touch from her gentle hand, soon wipes away my frown.

It's hard to recall all the things she's done, so of some I'll take my pick,
I think of days when I felt fed up, how she helped me when I was sick,
In days when I had self doubt, and would feel I couldn't cope,
She was always there beside me, to fill my life with hope.

If I could compare her to a temple, her heart would be the dome,
Her body would be the altar, her mind would make it a home,
For she is the brightness in my life, as gentle as a turtle dove,
The greatest gift she has for me, is the depth of her great love.

I do my best to return her love, yet I know that I am beat,
When I think of all her qualities, I know I can't complete,
Her love for me shines from her eyes, she fills my life with laughter,
She has the gift of healing hands, to compete I'd be a non starter.

Yet there again why should I compete, after all I'm only a man,
I'll do my best to make her happy, I'll do the best that I can,
In love I'm rich, I'm happy to say, her goodness is plain to see,
I also know why our marriage is strong, she works twice as hard as me.

This year like all the others, is the happiest that there has been,
If future years compare with the past, it's thanks to my dear Colleen,
I hope to make her happy in the years to come, I'll do the best that I can,
Yet it's possible you see, it won't be enough, after all I'm only a man.

*James T Wray*

## THE LOVERS

I suppose they tried their best, in many ways
I mean, through the sixties, the happy days
Married at sixteen, you know . . . when they had to
They lived by the boat, with the salt and shake
Both so busy, no time for a break.
          She's twenty-one now, both are so proud, with their
Expanding family, there's three now . . . a crowd.
He was a grafter, he worked with steel.
She was at home with the kids, and potatoes to peel.
          She's twenty-two now . . . with a new arrival,
Is it Stephen, is it Paul, they both choose the title.
They're happy now, or so they think . . .
Too many lies, despair and grief.
Neither think . . . I mean, well it hurts.
They're both still young and proud,
But they are both deceitful,
Too proud . . . to think aloud.
          She gets a job . . .
Well, it's a bad move.
When you are young, with freedom
Temptations flow strong . . .
Who knows, we never will, I suppose . . .
She was on the pill.
It hurt him . . . it would hurt anyone,
When suspicion arises, with your loved one.
The trust was gone . . . he had a go,
Next in line was the divorce proceedings . . . you know.
          The thing about it is, they still haven't learned,
Twelve years later . . . they're still getting burned.

*Tracie Deakin*

172

## REST ON, SWEET LOVE

Dream on, sweet love, and in thy dreams remember me:
For thee, in me, still livest thou;
In thy cold bed thou safest lie
No winds shall freeze; no summer's heat
Thy breath shall take; no thunder peal can now awake
Disturb thy rest, nor thee afright:
Thou sleepest safe in thine immortal world,
Dream on, sweet love, and in thy dreams remember me.

In me, thou wakest with each dawn:
In mine own ear thou hearest birds' sweet song
To greet the sunrise. Yet, bitter sweet
Such joy becomes that cannot share
With love the sweet content that once was there:
'Tis gone in mortal form yet deep within
Thy heart is there in eye, and thought, and prayer:
Sleep on, sweet love, and in thy dreams remember me.

Far o'er green fields sweet church bells ring,
In grey-stone church the faithful sing
Glad hymns that did thy soul uplift:
For thee they sing: still I am here to hear
The praises that you once did love:
Far above all earthly things in mind;
In thought; in faith, in hope and love:
They brought thee ease and comfort in thy troubled world.

My soul's with thee: for thee, in me, doth never leave:
Rest on, sweet love, and in thy rest remember me.

### *Wm A Palmer*

## SUPREME

Our magic wings of words
That speak its fill and clue
Both Nordic cupid through
And the Wales man reaches you.

At the mouth of love's mountain
Behind masks of hurt not hide.
Unburden the dry fountain
Letting go to explore - confide

Falling sagas's facade unfold
Between the lines looking at me,
Journeys gone cold
She and her king of the celtic sea.

Where we are in or go between
Harmony of voyagers in a dream
Prospering in a greater power

Where our words take to the wing
For no cause have I yours
Created this love-spring
That seizes my being
And your's mine
To make music supreme.

*David Lloyd-Howells*

## FIRST LOVE

You came into my life
When I was sweet sixteen
You brought within me a happy glow
That told me you I had to know.

You walked across the dance floor
You asked me to dance
With your arm around my waist and holding my hand
We glided together to the music of the band.

Each meeting was filled with excitement
Saturday couldn't come too soon
My knees would turn to jelly
When you walked in the room.

For a little while we had to part
Oh how it broke my teenage heart
But time passed and I look with joy
To a reunion with my teenage boy.

My heart beat fast when I saw you
You were near, I filled with joy
But someone else had her arms entwined
Around my teenage boy.

The sadness passed, we grew older
And went our separate ways
Years on now I remember
My first love of those teenage days.

*Winnie Milnes*

## YOU SAY

You say, my desire should be doubtless,
I'm in a safe-house cave-heart fascination, boundless,
You say (the one I love),
You never know my absolute intention, but
It's too black to mention, I can't explain;
Rutted and expressionless I remain . . .

You say 'Why do I always confer with walls?'
Naked thoughts run through rooms in my mind,
I'm spinning in confusion-lust, I mistrust myself, it seems;
You say,
I'm too distant for oneness or skin-tight emotional clams,
You took me, lifted me, and I, should I be found,
Now with nothing to compound, I can't convey my insanity or
My feelings, nearly or utterly in words,
The energy - effort fusion always goes unheard,
You say you need to know, why I don't love you so . . .

To me clarity is a non-communicable wisdom and all the fish jump from
                                                              the tank
You say I leave you dangling in circles of screams,
In sweaty, greasy ashtrays or unopened sweet-wrappers 'n dreams,
To you I'm the mouse on the moon, utterly crackers;

It's about some girl, I love her, I know,
I just can't seem to tell her so,
Devotion to her heart, it's tearing me apart
I'm too afraid of love's strange flesh, what the f*** is wrong with me,
I don't know where to start,
But I promise, to love thee, in my own way,
If not with dedication or sanity
Then poison-love ingots that banish me: to truth.

*David Jones*

## LEAVE-TAKING 1942

We stood upon the bridge love
And watched the river run
Then slowly wandered hand in hand
Towards the setting sun.
The fields soon damp with dewfall
Soft carpeted our feet
The carefree day was nearly done
And senses bittersweet.
As gentle breeze of twilight
Caressed like angel's breath
'Twas hard to think of conflict
Or blood, and tears and death.
The last of birdsong in the copse
Was music to our ears
The afterglow of sunset
A balm to quell our fears.
For we would soon be parting
Tomorrow you'd be gone
We needed this quiet memory
For dreams to dwell upon.
A blackout night descended
A bombers moon shone down
As arm about, you guided me
Homewards to the town.
And by my door beneath the stars
We said our fond goodbyes
And Oh . . . the ache remembering
The lovelight in your eyes..

*Marion P Webb*

## STAR STRUCK

Have you ever been in love
With someone on the Telly.
That made your mouth go dry
And put the jitters in your belly.

And when the show comes to an end
It's time to say 'Goodbye.'
The thought that you won't see his face
It makes you want to cry.

You capture him on video
Press pause to keep him still,
Rewind to watch him yet again
It gives you such a thrill.

Read everything about him
Watch every single show,
Fill your room with posters
Of your favourite Romeo.

You study him so closely
And you think you know him well,
But if you really met him
It would only break the spell.

You know you'll never meet him
Or ever hold his hands,
Yet he's the man in all your dreams
And no-one understands.

*Carol Prior*

## LITTLE STAR

The day you came into my life
my heart was filled with joy
I never would have guessed
one day I'd have a boy.

But you were oh so tiny
I couldn't take you home
the first five weeks of your life
I felt so all alone.

You've grown into a bonny lad
your beauty cannot hide
and every time I look at you
I'm bursting out with pride.

Your blonde hair and your blue eyes
So cheeky yet such fun
I thank a little star above
for giving me you son.

*Lesley Roscoe*


## THE SPLENDOUR OF YOUR LOVE

Holy spirit God of love, my heart
Is singing now, in the splendour
Of your love that every knee should bow.

In honour of your blessed name
Holy good and true, of the son
You sacrificed to reign on earth
For you.

In him there was no sin, he fought it
All with grace, in prayer he shed blood,
Sweat, and tears, eternal to be placed.

*Ruth McIntyre*

## LOVE IS

Love is as bright as the sun,
Love is loving your boyfriend's mum,
Love is sharing each other's thoughts,
Love is number one not noughts,
Love is as kind as the ocean blue,
Love is loving, loving you.

Love is gentle, love is kind,
Love is shouting if you don't mind,
Love should never ever die,
Love can sometimes make you cry,
Love is as kind as the ocean blue,
Love is loving, loving you.

Love is being who you are,
Loves is as golden as a star,
Love is spending time together,
Love is leaving no not never,
Love is as kind as the ocean blue,
Love is loving, loving you.

*Karen Jane Waite  (12)*


## MEET ME THERE, DEAR

Why do I never learn
Not to say
'Meet me there, dear?'
He'll lose his way.

I vow to myself,
Next time I'll remember
Not to say
'See you in a little while.'
He'll lose his way.

He'll always just think
Of something that seemed important.
He'll turn up,
When he's good and ready,
With a grin all over his face.

That's why I never remember
Not to say
'Meet me there, dear.'

*Felicity Minifie*

## LOVE LETTERS

Today I found the letters
In my drawer.
Under the lining, hidden
From prying eyes
Other than ours.
I'd forgotten how beautiful
Your words were
On paper, yellow with age,
You are still there, young,
In love with me and I with you.
The past will always remain
Unaltered by time.
And now I'm alone, our love stays
Alive in me,
Forever.

*Grace M Bexon*

## DUET

Within me dwells your heart.
A part of me and yet apart.
You're free and so am I,
Yet intertwined as one we fly
Through spaces, travelled not alone,
For each can call the other home.
There is no lock that seals this door,
For each is free just as before.
We strangers met and now are one.
Each of the other we've become.
And thus we know that should we part,
Deep each would stay in the other's heart.
And for us both a memory,
Duet in perfect harmony.

*Valerie Miles*

## REMEMBER WHEN

You have been my friend and guide
through life's stormy way
you are still a relative
you did not go astray.
memories are still as strong
of the love we have
even though age has upon us both become.

Remember, back to those early days
when we first became one
how serious about life we were
yet still had lots of fun:

Then bringing up the family
to be the best, suddenly
they grew up and we had a rest!
Now we ramble on, talking of the past
things we did together we were lucky, it did last.

Aye, time has its way
of bringing memories to the fore,
reminding one of passing days
things to be grateful for.

**Edith Mary Whamond**


## REMEMBER

Do you remember when we first met,
Or are you so disillusioned, you tried to forget.
Do you remember the girl, you danced round the floor,
And when you kissed her, her heart cried for more.
Do you remember when we could laugh,
       And when I was pregnant,
        We could still squeeze in a bath!
Do you remember the chocolates we shared,
When we lay, loving, in bed.
The laughter, the kisses, the happiness,
       And the words . . .
       That are no longer said.
Do you remember all these things,
       That we would love to do.
When I was so happy, just loving my Ted,
       And Ted loved his Muchy Moo!

**Sue Allison**

## TO MY WIFE JOAN
*(after 50 years of marriage)*

My darling wife, it must be said
I am so glad that we are wed
The love that brought us close together
Has grown apace whate'er the weather
We've had our ups and had our downs
We've had some smiles and had some frowns
We've had some highs we've had some lows
We've had some sunshine and some snows
We've had some sicknesses and health
We've shared our poverty and wealth
Everything we have is shared
For each other we have cared
Our children too have brought us joy
The last a girl, the first a boy
Now of course they too are grown
And both have families of their own
We cannot know what lies ahead
The years gone by seem to have sped
But, looking back across the years
With lots of smiles, and a few tears
We've shared the lot whate'er the weather
And thank our God we're still together
Whatever future years unfold
The secret we have must be told
*Togetherness* has been our theme
To work together as a team
We made our vows before the Lord
And always tried to keep our word
I thank my God in prayer each night
The Wife He chose for me was right.

**Horace Hartley**

184

## LOVE AND MY LONELY LIFE

It seems that in my lonely life, just for a little while
Love came my way,
Something so precious, but what one cannot buy,
Your love, like a blanket, enfolds me safe and warm,
The outside world can't hurt me -
With all its bitterness
Your hands, so warm and comforting, that hold me close and firm,
And eyes so full of love, and a mouth just waiting to be kissed.
Now I am complete,
To you, I am queen, beautiful, yet dainty and demure,
Sparkling, a gay companion, full of laughter.
I can forget the shy awkward being I was before you came
I look up, and see your sweet smiling face
So dear, and handsome, can you really be mine?
I've never asked for much dear Lord,
But this I pray,
Don't let a blot of human frailty
Spoil this heavenly love of mine,
Don't plunge me back into my narrow lonely world
That I endured before my darling came.

*Tomasine Oakley*

## MISSING YOU

A shadow on the stairway
A whisper in the night,
A face amongst the shoppers,
A half-remembered smile,
A life to live without you,
A path to tread alone,
A step or two behind me,
Always out of reach.

*Rosemary Jennings*

## ALL THE MAN THAT I NEED

A kiss fresh and new
a smile for me alone
we wake together
to greet the day

When you're asleep
I lie awake
wrapped in your arms
I have to touch you
making sure you're there
to check you're really mine

In case you're stolen
from me
while I sleep
my arms are wrapped tight around you
Each time I look at you
it's like
seeing you for the first time
You're the only man I want
and the only man I need

*S A Hoggard*

## SWAIN OR SWINE?

What fulsome praise
Thou doth bestow,
With words as sweet as honey,
Pray tell me more for yes or no,
Methinks thou wants my money.

*Mary Haslam*

## JEANNIE

I first beheld thee,
With a poet's eye.
A gift which I possess,
But had it been
With a soldier's gaze
I would not have loved thee less.

If I'd been a thief, or sailor man,
Or a gypsy
Roaming free.
Or a beggar man sitting,
Bowl in hand
My love would still be thee.

If I'd a tailor or cobbler been,
Or rustic farmer
At the plough.
*My* love, you would have always been,
True then and still true now.

*John Bracken*


## LOVE

As sunlight on a distance golden glows
Within a palisade, a wall of shadows
As on a kingdom brightly set apart,
So you came silently upon my heart.

So quietly, I knew it not, yet found
In wonder, showering me around
A golden light of love that did not fade
And stood within the kingdom you had made.

*Muriel E Bowman*

## LOVE'S QUEST

Elusive now the joy that once
     Leapt to my heart unbidden
In my life's quest are such sweet things
     To be forever hidden
Long though I've searched and cannot find
     That which I once knew well
Away, away, went all my bliss
     Whence I cannot tell
Could such brief rapture then impart
     In humble life like mine
A heart that hopes to find once more
     And know, such love divine.

*Jeannette Facchini*

## AWAKE AT 3 AM

Roused, I gaze at you slumbering -
3am and deep in sleep so sound.
Long dark lashes tight to cheek
Covering green eyes; bright and round.

Awake; lovingly I watch you dormant -
Darkest night lit by lamp glowing
Your smile in repose - no laughter lines.
Sensual pink lips gently parting.

Conscious; I softly touch your face
Erythritic stubble a fuzz on your chin.
Tousled hair upon the pillow.
What did I do you to win?

*Catriona Morrison*

## STROLLING ON THE BEACH

I walk alone beside the sea
My feet on golden sand,
You are not here to stroll with me
And gently hold my hand,
The waves are singing our refrain
As in and out they flow,
The song you always sang to me
I'll always love you so.

As I look up to the heavens
The seagulls screech to me,
They glide up in the sky so high
So happy to be free,
As I watch the children play
Their laughter in my ears,
They don't even notice me
My eyes so full of tears.

I see a ship upon the sea
And watch it disappear,
Is it going to distant lands
Or off to somewhere near,
As my eyes turn again to heaven
I wonder if you can see,
The little speck upon the beach
Yes darling it is me.

*Muriel P Cooper*

## FOR THE ONE I LOVE

I love
Anything and anybody that centre on *me* -
Acclaim, applause, approval, admiration;
Dotage, cooing and billing (but not invoicing);
Plenty of physical love; stroking, caressing,
Sweet words, kindness, gentleness, softness;
Sensation, stimulation, excitement, passion;
Climaxes, relief, release, freedom;
Earth, air, sky, water;
The mountains, the sea, the forests, the hills,
The valleys, the plains, the land;
Rich, brown soil, pebbles, stones, boulders;
The minutae of life
Beneath, above, below, around;
Everywhere, everything and everybody;
I love, I love, I love;
Pain, suffering, hardship;
Even death itself,
I love,

(signed)

*God!*

*Howard Kaye*


## THIS LOVE DID FIND US

If we had met when we were young
- and yet, we lived and loved,
Enjoyed the things we did
The friends we were among -

We could have held hands, touched,
As we do now and warmed
To all the hidden thoughts
And tenderness that formed

In such a short sweet time. Not lost!
Though innocence has fled
And youth did disappear,
But nothing did it cost.

For now I am repaid
One hundredfold and blessed
With overwhelming joy
By loving arms caressed.

No yearning now for years long spent,
On other joys or bliss
That came and went with time.
For this love were we meant.

And age will just enhance
This pleasure which is ours.
Pray, may we dwell awhile
The wonder ever flowers.

*Les Pearce*


## LADYWOOD

We went one night, to Ladywood, to find the wishing-stone,
        (you only see it when the moon is round).
I knew if we should find it, that we wouldn't be alone
        (an old Grey-Lady guards her haunting-ground).

But love was strong that evening, and cast out all our fear;
        we found the stone, and sealed our wish of love,
Then wandered slowly homeward, past the deep and silent mere,
        at ease with all the ghosts in heaven above.

I knew our lovers' wish that night, was certain to come true,
        For, as we climbed across the broken stile,
I turned around and blew a kiss of happiness to you,
        and saw the old, Grey-Lady faintly smile.

*Shirley Frances Winskill*

## HELEN

Although we are so far apart
I can feel the beating of your heart,
I can touch your lips and feel your hair
But when I open my eyes, I see nothing there . . .
So, hands in pockets, I strode sadly on
For my vision of you had surely gone.
I stop to ponder, I wrack my brain,
I close my eyes, it's there again . . .
Now how is this, can it be true?
I see a picture my darling of you
Am I a victim of some cruel joke,
Or has my imagination run amok?
Sometimes I can't quite understand
How your visions comes at my command,
But I think this can only be
Because I wish so hard that you were here with me . . .

*Brian Ducker*


## LOVE EVERLASTING

The only sound is my heartbeat;
Mingling with your whispered sighs:
As we stroll through *Moonlit Shadows*,
Under stars in indigo skies!

Naive and young, only in our teens . . .
Our *first kiss* and my heart skips a beat:
This surely is *Paradise* . . .
Treading *Stardust* 'neath our feet!

We stand for a while by an oak tree;
Enraptured by nightingale song;
So aware of *the magic* of *new love* . . .
But to *indulge* . . . premarriage; . . . *so wrong*!

*Here* . . . all round us; . . . *wonderful music?*
In *this ambience* . . . *so very apt:*
Relative to Rudolfo/Mimi's tender duet;
Transcending *to moments* . . . so rapt!

Misty-eyed and tremulous. . .
*Both pledged our love* . . . Devout!
A *Love* to sustain . . . whate'er in store:
Of that we have no doubt!

**Gertrude Cuthbertson-Parsons**


## THE RETURN

'I've come back, and I'll stay a while,' I smiled.
She wept, wiped eyes with her shawl, but watched,
And in watching, my soul was fresh beguiled.
She sniffed. 'Ha, lovers' tiffs? Eros debauched?'

We'd argued so fierce and made up so sweet,
Too often, too soon, excitement in fear.
Our wars lengthened, 'though make up became fleet,
Stone words used in haste, sour-chosen to sear.

'Yes, my love, that's all to it,' I answered.
'While a gift, more precious than jewels lies ours.
Unguarded, not enhanced, but not yet dead.
By squabbling, black ice smothers its flowers.'

She spoke once more, to toss back my own words,
'Don't stand in the chill,' and swung the gate wide.
Words of warmth these, safe in scabbards, the swords,
Our ark launched, reckless, on Valentine's tide.

**Jim Easton**

# HAPPY ANNIVERSARY

Flowers and cards
For momentous days,
Once every year
Then they fade away.

Many loving years we claim,
By sailing along
Through night and day,
The love we found, we have today.

No need for cards
To demonstrate,
The love we have
Is with truth and faith.

The vows we made,
They still relate,
The true love we had
We still hold today.

So stop and think,
Throughout the years,
The fruits of life
You helped to bear.

No words of man,
Not with flowers or cards,
Can express my true feelings,
I hold, for you in my heart.

***Norrie Hill***

## OVER THE MOON

I'm over the moon, I'm so happy
There's no need for wherefores or whys
It's there in my smile, in my big beaming smile
And it's there in the stars in my eyes.

I wake up each morning so happy
And I smile to the ceiling above
I wave to the calendar hung on the wall
And shout aloud, 'I am in love.'

I'm in love with a girl in a million
And she loves me right back, glory be
She's gorgeous, she's lovely, a darling
There's no-one as lucky as me.

We're married, oh yes, we are married
And we have been for some little time
The day that my sweetheart said shyly 'I do'
Was the day my life reached the sublime!

Now I'm going to share a small secret
And friend, you can take it as read
Tomorrow is our anniversary
And we shall be forty years wed.

I'm still over the moon, I'm so happy
I'm living a wonderful life
You can see right away why I feel like I do
I'm still madly in love with my wife!

*Joe Silver*

## AUTUMN LOVE

The last hill climbed, my days now few,
      A blessing God has sent to me.
Bathed by autumn sun and morning dew,
      The last rose of summer he gave to me.

To fall in love in autumn years,
      When one's life is all but told;
Silent prayers, reward for tears,
      A gift from God of purest gold.

'Twas a gentle, kind and loving man
      Reached out his hand to me.
Melted my heart and tears began
      Inward, deep - such ecstasy!

Each precious hour each precious day,
      We comfort, share and understand.
God bless our love we humbly pray,
      As we tread our last days - hand in hand.

*Barbara Southern*




## NOW THAT I HAVE FOUND YOU

I searched the seas to find your heart,
I searched the skies to find your winged spirit,
I touched the moon to find your universe
and I found a shining star.
I have you in the palms of my hands
like a butterfly, gently caressed
in vivid colours of love.
When I let you fly
you are the soul of paradise
shining down on me.

*Julie Mears*

# I WOULD MARRY YOU TOMORROW

I was fifteen, you a year older, on the night we met,
At a dance - that evening is one I never will forget.
You said you looked round for the prettiest girl there;
I wore my best dress and had curled my blonde hair.

We fell in love and courted four years, walking for miles,
Talking, laughing and kissing, you lifted me over stiles.
When we planned to marry, you asked for my father's consent;
With our simple village church wedding, we were so content.

No honeymoon for us - our home had consumed our money.
We didn't have luxuries, nor did we expect bread and honey.
You a miner, me a nurse, we worked hard and for long hours.
Many household items were second hand, but paid for, ours.

I became pregnant unexpectedly, naively, straight away.
When our daughter was born, weren't we excited that day?
Heads down, in a carrier bag, you brought me carnations.
That night, you and your mates joined in celebrations.

When our baby son arrived, you were as proud as punch;
You walked in with blue irises, arranged in a proper bunch.
Both our offspring's wedding days we recall with pleasure.
We have two wonderful grandchildren to love and treasure.

Ups and downs we've gone through, storms and sunny weather,
Sometimes even wondering if we would survive together.
Yet here we are, having known each other thirty-two years;
Love, joy and laughter have mingled with fights and tears.

We've had to have patience, tolerance and forgiveness too,
But I can say with certainty, you love me and I love you.
We have grown up together amid our good times and sorrow
And, my darling Valentine, I would marry you again tomorrow.

*Janet Hewitt*

# RECOLLECTIONS

I recall your ever present sincerity,
no word spoken in haste without meaning,
no gushing sentiments leaving questions unanswered.
I recall your ever present caring and gentleness,
when most needed at traumatic moments,
at times when shared thought and understanding
dissolves difficulty.
After all the years together I feel these sentiments
at present.
I am sitting with you now, we are looking far
across Exmoor acres.
No words are being spoken, we have no need;
We are content within a world that would benefit
from this total inner quiet.

*Lesley M Eldred*


# UNSPOKEN LOVE

I hear your voice, and a thousand feelings surge along my veins.
I see your smile and know it's meant for me.
I hear your words, and like your smile, they wear a veil
That only we can set aside when none can see . . .

We share our thoughts, with not a word to show
How close we've grown as joys and tears we've shared -
But warmth there is, that gives my heart a glow
When you're not there . . .

When you're not there, and other love you share
I, too share love with those around who care;
But there are times when precious moments rare
Bring us together - and the air is fresh and light -
And *you* are there . . .

*Frances Alder*

198

# CHILDHOOD SWEETHEARTS

Sharing chips watching the sea.
Sat on park benches covered in coats.
Laughing at anything.
Nervous but happy.
Phoning for no reason.
First to answer their door.
Last home from school.
Rushing the homework.
Suddenly not hungry.
Watching the clock.
Keeping secrets from classmates.
Avoiding parents questions,
Holding hands in the dark.
Scribbled messages when plans change.
Lonely at bed time
Washing more carefully.
Using the spot cream.
Hair gels and body spray.
Making plans.
Wanting to be alone.
Emotional softness.
Frightened hearts.
Childish giggles.
Adult games.
Promises to keep.
Hearts to break.
But it wasn't mine.
And it wasn't yours.
From childhood sweethearts.
To adult lovers.

*Dewi Wyn Hughes*

## BELOVED

What can I say
most dearly loved
that will at all convey
the inmost feeling of my heart
now that you're away?

Should I reveal
most well beloved,
in this deep loneliness
the single thought upon my mind
is of your tenderness.

Shall I admit
my dearest dear,
that when I am alone
I am but only half alive
so close we've grown?

Gladly I say
adored one,
you are everything to me,
your smile my sun
your love my ecstasy!

*Joan Miles Lister*


## SUNDAY AFTERNOON

And as the fading sun allows the hearth to glow,
the hissing logs and pulsing embers smile,
their welcome blush pervades each corner of the room
and cloaks the afternoon in bygone style.

Though coffee cups lie empty on the table top,
the taste of Sunday roast remains to tease,
and Tabby's purr vibrates with mute ferocity
while strains of Elgar drift with timeless ease.

If I could sew I'd curl up with my tapestry
and work the fabric and the thread with flair,
and if you smoked you'd slumber with your favourite pipe,
enticing pungent whispers through the air.

Yes, I forewent the chance to travel far and wide
and paint the town a vibrant reddish hue.
I spurned the eye of many who would take my hand
to spend my Sunday afternoons with you.

*Rachel Webb*


## 25 YEARS ON

Oh name that makes me tremble,
Oh lips that make me sigh,
There's no question why I love you
I know the reason why.
You've been so kind and gentle,
Upheld me through the years.
We've shared such happy laughter
And cried some bitter tears.
But throughout our chosen journey
On life's tempestuous sea,
I've never had to worry,
You're always there for me.
Best friend and gentle lover
Strong arm and shoulder soft,
With you beside me all these years
I've never once felt lost.
I'll always love you dearly
Until the end of life.
I'm so happy and so thankful,
You chose me for your wife.

*Jennie Schofield*

## THE CORNER OF MY AVENUE

The days dragged
Between those precious hours I spent with you
- Then you'd turn the corner -
Your smile on seeing me
Sent my senses soaring - every time -
You reached out as I ran towards you
And all I could ever do
Was close my eyes and savour
The delight of that always perfect kiss.
Oh, how I loved you then.
You touched my cheek
I kissed your hand
So much to say
But nothing said.
Just walking with you
Those early springtime evenings
left my body weak with longing.
And as I lay with you
I knew this was for always.
Memories glimmer paler now
of more than forty years ago.
But oh so clearly
Do I see you turn that corner
That from then, till now
There is nothing in between.

*Sylvia Cox*

**IF I COULD . . .**

If I could live my life again
        I wouldn't change a single day
As long as you were there beside me
        Every step of my life's way

I'd count my blessings one by one
        I'd count my troubles too
Though they seem so incidental now
        For I've shared them all with you

Your lips that shine . . . your eyes that smile . . .
        Your tend warm caress
Complement the inner glow
        That holds your gentleness

If I could just put into words
        How much you mean to me
I'd write the longest poem by far
        To let my feelings free

If I could show the way I feel
        I'd show sweet yesterdays
When your love touched a thousand times
        In many many ways

If I could feel each silver touch
        And live each golden memory
I'd show you heaven will be here
        Now and for eternity . . .

*Norm Whittle*

## KISSES

Lingering ones, passionate ones, there's nothing like kissing
If you don't indulge you don't know what you're missing

Kissing can be intimate, kissing can be fun
But you need a partner cause it's useless as one

A French kiss, a smacker or a quick peck
Try them all and it's great on the neck

Let your lips wander and go with the flow
From the tips of the fingers down to the big toe

*Sarah Humphries*


## DESIRE

Your eyes glisten so brightly
Your mouth is tender and warm
I embrace you close and hold you tightly
And now a new love is born

Your beating heart now races
Your tendering hands can touch
Eye to eye we near our faces
And I have what I've wanted so much

I calm in your loving arms
I'm breathless at your desire
I'm taken in by all your charms
Our love is a raging fire.

*Jacqui Simkin*

## THE LITTLE THINGS

It's just the little things you do,
that make me understand,
the way your eyes look at me,
the way you hold my hand.

It's just the little things you say,
the words that make me smile,
and all the love you give to me,
that makes my life worthwhile.

It's just the little thoughts you give,
that show me that you care,
the times of tears and sadness,
the fears we have to share.

It's just your little annoyances,
the one's that I ignore,
the good that outshines the bad,
that makes me love you more.

It's just the little things in life,
that you say and do
which makes me realise
how much I really love you.

*J E Millar*


## UNTITLED

You comfort me when I am sad
You make me laugh when things are bad
You bring the sun into my life
You banish all my grief and strife
You give me lots of tenderness too
And that is why I love you.

*B Woolrich*

## ALL THIS TIME

I've know you for about a year
and slowly I overcame my fear
of trusting you, falling in love
of you being all I dream of
I felt so vulnerable and very weak,
yet still it was always you I'd seek.
You can be brash but you're funny, gentle and kind
You're all those things I wanted but could never find.
You were there right there in front of me
yet stubbornly I refused to see
I tried to hate you for so long
I thought it would work, but I was wrong.
I realised you'd hidden your better side
Your immaturity was only on the outside.
Now I know I can love again,
I know you won't cause me any pain
It's funny how before we barely spoke to each other
then the atmosphere started to change between us forever.
We still have a long way to go
but it's working and we both know
We're beginning to like each other now
I don't know why, it doesn't matter how
It's in your eyes and mine
this feeling that developed in time.
We're drawn together like a moth to the light
whenever I'm near you something feels so right
With you in my mind I'm no longer alone
With you in my heart I'm finally home.
We're destined to fit together like hand and glove
I thought I hated you, yet all this time, I was falling in love.

*Hannah Prosser*

## LONGINGS

You never really talk to me these days,
And when I speak, you never really hear;
The words that pass between us float around
Like fragile bubbles in a silent void.

And yet, I love you still.

You never really touch me any more,
And when I reach for you, you turn away;
We don't hold hands, or walk out arm in arm,
We only kiss at Christmas and New Year.

And yet, I love you still.

You long since ceased to ask me what I think,
And never, now, enquire how I feel;
My days of joy, or sorrow, or despair,
No longer stir the interest of concern.

And yet, I love you still.

But if you think the same is true of me,
And I am just as guilty, in your eyes,
Than all I ask is, every night, like me,
Hold fast to this - the truth that matters most.

You love me still.

*Jean Scott*

## I STILL REMEMBER YOU

The water lapped around me as
I stood quite still on sandy shore.
Alone was I with just my thoughts
And wishing you were there once more.

We'd walked together on the beach
And stood beneath the star lit sky.
I gazed at it much paler now
And never knew the reason why.

The precious love we once had known.
The joy of everything we shared
Had turned to emptiness and pain,
And in the silence I despaired.

I watched the gulls wheel overhead
Then settle on the cliffs above.
They seemed content for life went on,
But where were you and where was love?

My happiness on wings had flown
Like birds departing from the nest.
The bridegroom quietly waiting still.
The wedding feast without a guest.

The wind was echoing around.
I felt it gently brush my face
And touch the stinging moisture there.
My tears of pity not of grace.

The sadness clung to my poor heart.
This tortured soul, such grief it knew.
Dear love, my love, where have you gone?
Sweet love I still remember you.

*John Christopher Cole*

## NO REGRETS

I wish I had my life again,
I then would leave out some of the pain,
The struggles and strife of being a wife,
For part and all and the whole of my life.
I tried too hard to treat them fair,
As playing part of mother,
That in this life you have to share,
Not one against the other.

For all the problems up and down,
We shared together all we found,
The good, the bad,
The happy, the sad,
The way we both were taught,
When either one distraught.
To stop and think and then to pray,
For the choice I had of another.
I married the man I am glad to say,
Is not like any other!

*Marlene M Gilbert*


## EARLY FEBRUARY

Once again I returned to the Mediterranean.
I immersed myself in cold water
And chased fish along the sandy beds.

I found an islet where only sea
Birds had left footprints. I wanted
So much that you were there.

On such a day I realised
Life relies on being filled with joy.
I knew then I would live with you.

*Robert James Carr*

## PAUL

I think you're really special
I love those blue eyes of yours
You only have to look at me
And I'll keep coming back for more.

When we are together
I love to hold you tight
You make me feel secure
You make everything all right.

But what I'm trying to tell you
Is you are so full of life and zest
You make the world a happier place
I'm lucky I've got the best.

*Jackie Stallabrass*


## FLO TIME

Of this month - its days containing
Thoughts and looks and words of Flo,
Therefore in my heart remaining
E'en if years entire should go -

            I would halt each minute's fleetness,
            Make each moment last for two,
            Just because your love, your sweetness
            Cause me to be born anew.

I would bid each day to linger,
Lasting like two days - or three.
Fate stretched forth her kindest finger
When she guided you to me,
So I ask her not to sever
Bonds that truly bind us fast
But to stay as kind as ever,
Making even seconds last . . .

*Peter S A Cooper*


## LET ME STEAL YOUR HEART

Let me steal your heart tomorrow,
You will never know that it's gone,
You can just carry on,
And if I steal a kiss, in the mist,
While walking in the rain,
Will you complain,
You won't feel any pain, you won't feel any sorrow,
If I steal your heart tomorrow,
Let me steal your heart,
And fly you around, the heavens and the stars
Maybe while we are out in space,
We could visit Mars,
If you let me steal your heart tomorrow,
If I steal your heart tomorrow,
Your laughter will be heard,
Beneath the stars, carried by the wind,
And echoed by the birds,
I will know the reason why,
You have that twinkle in your eye,
If I steal your heart tomorrow.

*R Scoot*

## TWO HEARTS BEATING AS ONE

Two hearts beating as one
In perfect harmony
Until our time is done
A beacon for all to see

We fell in love in our teens
No other thoughts in our minds
Each in each other's dreams
A love like no other kind

Growing closer through the years
Taking knocks and falls
Staying together and shedding tears
Surviving through close calls

Thinking as one as time went by
Knowing our minds were in tune
Seeing things eye to eye
As the earth does with the moon

Always presenting a united stand
No chink in our armour to impose
Walking through life hand in hand
No secrets for others to expose

Soul mates ready for the hereafter
True love as bright as the sun
Two spirits sharing laughter
Two hearts beating as one.

*Dave Melbourne*

## HE'S ALWAYS THERE

This poem is dedicated to the one I love
Who was sent to me on the wings of a dove
He's always there when help I need
To smooth my brow or sow a seed
He's always there when I'm down and blue
To show me the light and pull me through
He's always there when things go wrong
To make me laugh or sing a song
He's also there in rain or sun
When I'm being lazy or on the run
Ever there to make me smile or wipe away my tears
Calming me down and quelling my fears
He's also there to share a walk
Sit in silence or when I want to talk
He's there too for a wander in the park
Or to hold my hand when it's getting dark
Always there to share my stress or laughter
And long may it stay so for our happy ever after
My constant protector . . . a knight amongst men
For whom I thank God and add Amen.

*Cherry Somers-Dowell*

## WILL YOU MARRY ME?

I can't imagine life without you
I need to be with you all the time
Put your arms around me, and
Please be forever mine.

I've never felt like this before
I can't believe I've found you at last
I'm so happy to be near you
Heartache and tears are all in the past.

Our love is something special
We share and laugh together
Your smile is etched on my mind
Let's make it last forever.

You're all I've ever wanted
Please don't set me free.
I will always love you.
Will you marry me?

*Maria Brown*


## MAGIC

The air is sweet,
The night is young,
And we've only just began.

The sky is salmon pink,
The clouds burst,
Into a diamond shower,
Which stab at the land,
By the hour.

Then all is still,
And a bird paints a picture,
With a merry shrill.

We sit,
Wet to the bone,
And the magic,
Is all our own.

*Sandra J Middleton*


## TOGETHER AS ONE

You are me, I am you
We are together as one,
No longer apart
No longer alone
We have found love
Together as one,
To part would be to die
I cannot breathe without you
Without you, I shall not live
You give me life
You give me love
You don't always know it
We both seldom show it,
But we are together as one,
Today, tomorrow, forever
We shall always be,
We are together as one
For now and forever,
We breathe for each other
We will always be together as one.

*Niki Foxwell*

## VISION IN A DREAM

I dream of my one true love
An angel sent from heaven above
A voice as smooth as birds in the sky
As gentle as clouds floating by
As romantic as candles burning bright
Beautiful as the ocean in full moonlight
As pure and as kind, as a dove
This man of my dreams, wants me to love
He's as soft as whispers of waves on the shore
And handsome, like I've never seen before
As strong as a log fire burning bright
But calm as a river in the still of the night
Such thoughts give out a loving theme
This man, an angel in every girl's dream . . .

*Christine Nicholson*

## SONG FOR LOST LOVERS

This is a song for all lost lovers,
Forgotten, in the neglect of years -
A tear or two for the old days,
When a kiss stole a beat from your heart;
All that remains of yesterday's dreams
Is the pain when lovers part.

This is a song for all lost lovers,
For the final parting, the last adieu -
A tear or two for the old days,
When a kiss farewell tasted bitter-sweet;
Now remembering yesterday's dreams
Two lost lovers meet . . .

*Gaelyn Jolliffe*

## THAT'S WHY I LOVE YOU SO

Whenever I feel lonely,
Somehow you're always there.
Whenever I am troubled,
Somehow I know you care.
There's no-one else in all the world
With whom I'd rather go
Along life's long and winding road,
That's why I love you so.

Whenever I am happy,
You are happy too.
And when I want to share my thoughts
I share them all with you,
And when at times I lose my way
You point the way to go.
With you, the world's a wonderful place
That's why I love you so.

*E Julia Horton*

## MY VALENTINE

Skilled writers and great poets have written verse and prose
Comparing love with music, or like a deep red rose.
But we know love is precious and we know that its worth
Can't be compared with anything that's to be found on earth.

For you have known great sadness, upon life's waves been tossed,
And felt the pain of suffering with loved ones you have lost.
Now, days are full of sweetness, you're free from all alarms,
For you have found a shelter dear, within my loving arms.

I had been oh so lonely, and longed to share a home.
But felt, just like a mariner on stormy seas - alone.
But when a storm is over, and the sun shines from above,
So I have come to rest, in the harbour of your love.

The majesty of mountains, and the mystery of the sea,
The cool shade in a summer wood, that's what you are to me.
For you are just the strength I need, when I am tired and weak,
You stand so strong and resolute, the safety that I seek.

Like the sunshine of each day that dawns, our gold along life's path.
The sweet peace of contentment that we find beside our hearth.
These then are our riches, a happy carefree home
Where seeds of laughter, trust and love forever have been sown.

And so you have this heart of mine
My husband dear, *my valentine.*

**Angela Douse**

## ALL THE TREASURES

All the treasures of the world are mine
The secret of this joy divine
Lies in the beauty of your eyes
The warm deep timbre of your voice
The intricacies of your desires

Strength; in your hands, gentle and fine
Your arms of steel
Your body, hard, so hard, for me
Yet in the answer to my plea
A soft luxurious resting place

Oh! I am dizzy with this wine, intoxicated with fire and heat
Brought to me by this wine so sweet, which stems from love, brings ecstasy
Eternally will I drink from this cup of life
This cup of life is you.

You entrance me taunt me with your whims
With your exquisite torments you will ever hold my trust heart
Without a need of chains or vice. Yet as two lonely songbirds skim
So swift - oh, heaven sent, across the morning air
So far apart are you and I. But it is somehow wise
To secrete a precious thought, retain an atom of individuality
Whilst giving all, whilst being one.
Oh his, a dream of paradise, as thick as honey, clear as ice
Each feeling one which penetrates, no compromise, no shadows
All awareness, sweet perception, piercing, singing, shouting, sobbing
We are the sun, the universe
So great, magnificent and golden, a golden burst of glory, molten
showering the mundane earth with living joy.
And now, green, cool, so dark, a scented gloom, deep ever deep
A peace before unknown to man. In this forever we will sleep.

*Janice Hunter*

## GALATEA

She lies
Pale on the rumpled
Whiteness of the bed,
Her body moving slowly
With breathing sleep
Upon her, a second skin
Of sweat, the day outside
A heavy daze of heat,
And she is smiling
The reason hidden
Behind her silent eyes
The curtain of her hair
Dark flung on the pillow;
Music plays far away
She is its rhythm and
Its harmonies echo in her
I lean my head against
Her gentle breast
And hear her heart
Soft and strong, shadow
Of laughter within;
Yet I know that I
Can't hold her always,
I place a dark rose
Upon her smooth white skin
And kiss her into life.

*S D Weber*

# INFORMATION

We hope you have enjoyed reading this book - and
that you will continue to enjoy it in the coming years.

If you like reading and writing poetry drop us a line,
or give us a call, and we'll send you a free information
pack.

Poetry Now Information
1-2 Wainman Road
Woodston
Peterborough
PE2 7BU